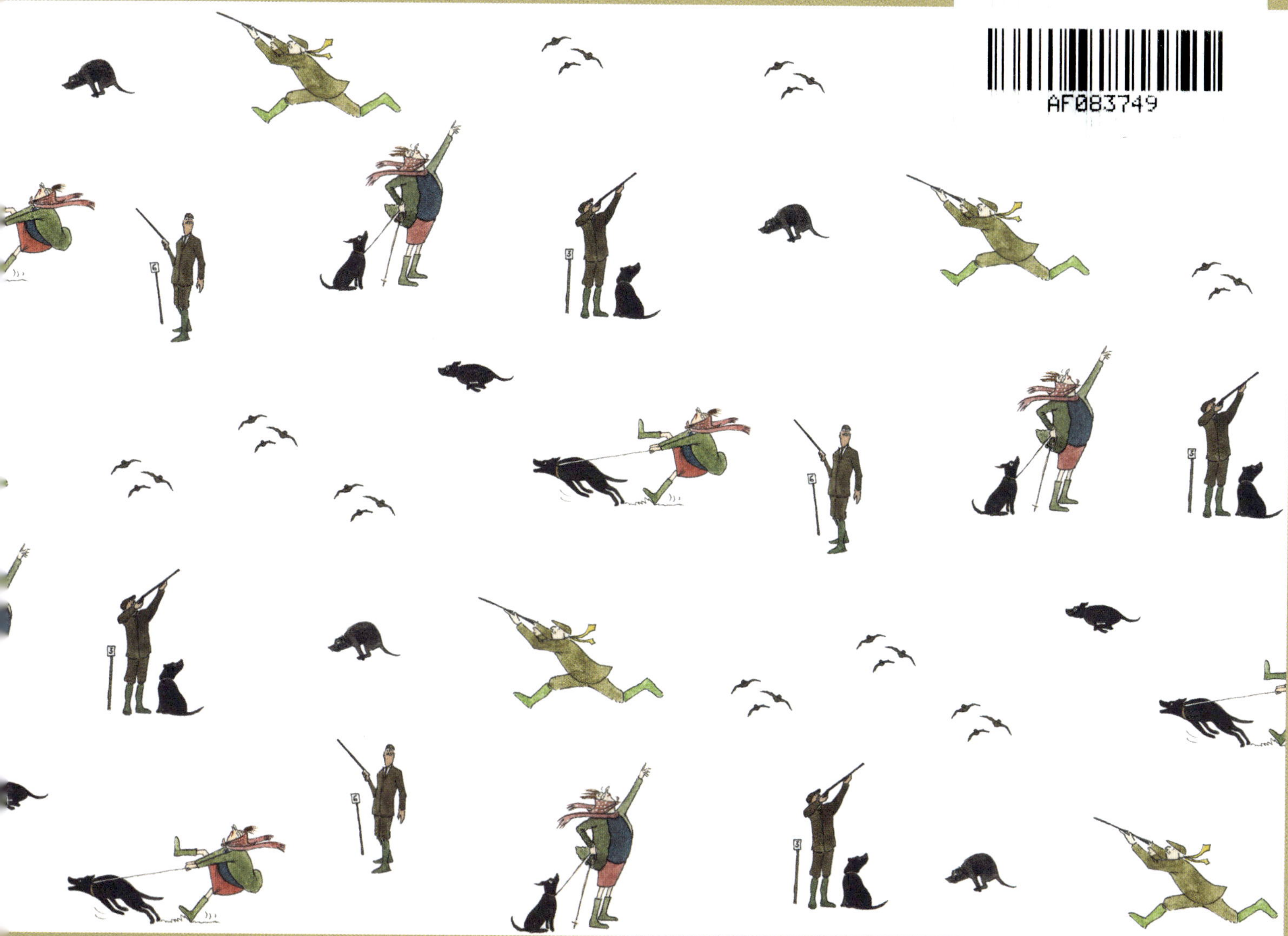

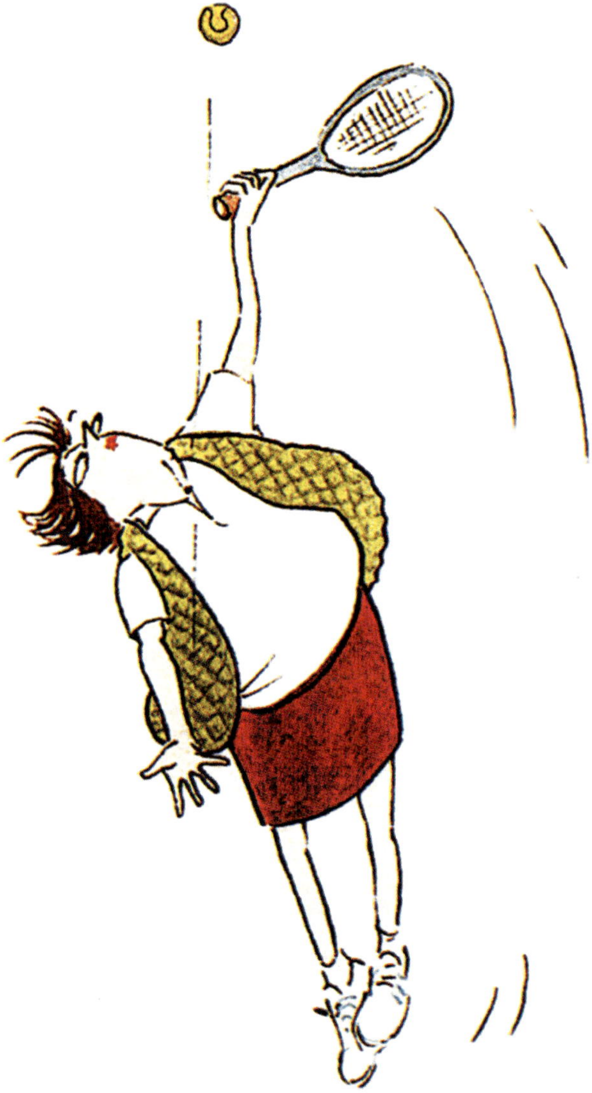

TOTTERING-BY-GENTLY®

FUN AND GAMES with the Totterings

ANNIE TEMPEST

Quiller

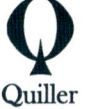

Copyright © 2024 The O'Shea Gallery
Text and illustrations copyright © 2024 Annie Tempest
Illustrations archived and compiled by Raymond O'Shea

First published in the UK in 2024 by Quiller,
an imprint of Amberley Publishing

British Library Cataloguing-in-Publication Data
A catalogue record for this book is available from the British Library.

Hardback ISBN 978 1 84689 405 3
E-book ISBN 978 1 84689 406 0

The right of Annie Tempest to be identified as the author of this work has been asserted in accordance with the Copyright, Design and Patent Act 1988.

All rights reserved. No part of this book may be reproduced or transmitted in any form or by any means, electronic or mechanical including photocopying, recording or by any information storage and retrieval system, without permission from the Publisher in writing.

The images featured in this book are available as prints from www.tottering.com

Printed in China

Quiller
An imprint of Amberley Publishing Ltd
The Hill, Merrywalks, Stroud GL5 4EP
Tel: 01453 847800
Email: info@quillerbooks.com
Website: www.quillerpublishing.com

ANNIE TEMPEST

Annie Tempest is one of the top cartoonists working in the UK. This was recognised in 2009 with the Cartoon Art Trust awarding her the Pont Award for the portrayal of the British character. Annie's cartoon career began in 1985 with the success of her first book, *How Green Are Your Wellies?* This led to a regular cartoon, 'Westenders' in the *Daily Express*. Soon after, she joined the *Daily Mail* with 'The Yuppies' cartoon strip which ran for more than seven years and for which, in 1989, she was awarded Strip Cartoonist of the Year. Since 1993 Annie Tempest has been charting the life of Daffy and Dicky Tottering in 'Tottering-by-Gently' – the phenomenally successful weekly cartoon strip in *Country Life*.

Daffy Tottering is a woman of a certain age who has been taken into the hearts of people all over the world. She reflects the problems facing women in their everyday life and is completely at one with herself, while reflecting on the intergenerational tensions and the differing perspectives of men and women, as well as dieting, ageing, gardening, fashion, food, field sports, convention and much more.

Daffy and her husband Dicky live in the fading grandeur of Tottering Hall, their stately home in the fictional county of North Pimmshire, with their extended family: daughter Serena, and grandchildren, Freddy and Daisy. The daily, Mrs Shagpile, and the love of Dicky's life, Slobber, his black Labrador, and the latest addition to the family, Scribble, Daisy's working cocker spaniel, also make regular appearances.

Annie Tempest was born in Zambia in 1959. She has a huge international following and has had numerous one-woman shows all over the world during her thirty-five-plus years as a cartoonist. Over the last decade she has emerged as a sculptor as well, using her knowledge of body language from her years of observation in this new medium. Simply, people interest Annie and nothing escapes her gimlet eye. *Fun and Games with the Totterings* is published in celebration of Annie's cartoon strip 'Tottering-by-Gently' appearing in *Country Life* magazine for the past thirty years and gives Tottering fans a glimpse into the sporting pursuits and pastime activities of Britain's leading cartoon aristocrats.

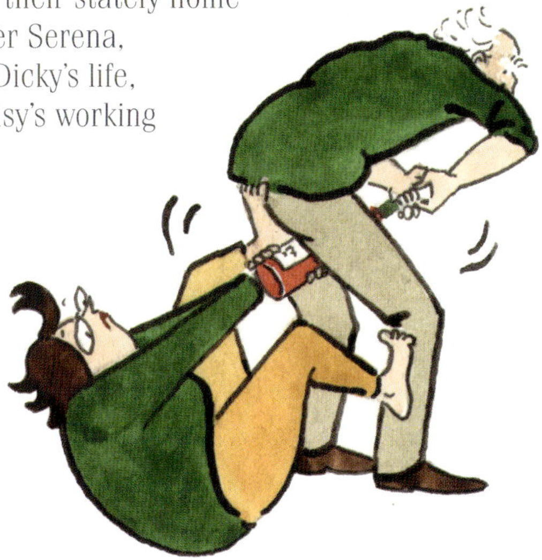

FOREWORD

The Totterings have been appearing on the final page in *Country Life* and both delighting and charming the readers for so long that it comes as a surprise to find that they were not in the first issue of the magazine in 1897.

Together with the frontispiece, 'Tottering-by-Gently' perfectly bookends *Country Life*'s eclectic mix of articles and spellbinding imagery. Few starts and finishes to a magazine can have given more pleasure. Indeed, the Duke of Devonshire once wrote that everyone read *Country Life* from back to front because of Annie Tempest's brilliance.

The publication of this volume, *Fun and Games with the Totterings*, means that there are now more than twenty books featuring this charismatic and amusing family, to go along with the thousands of cartoon strips that have been printed each week in the magazine.

I often marvel at how Annie Tempest comes up with a new idea every week, but we are all so thrilled she does so, as her brilliant evocations of life at Tottering Hall, as well as her wit and wisdom, bring a jot more

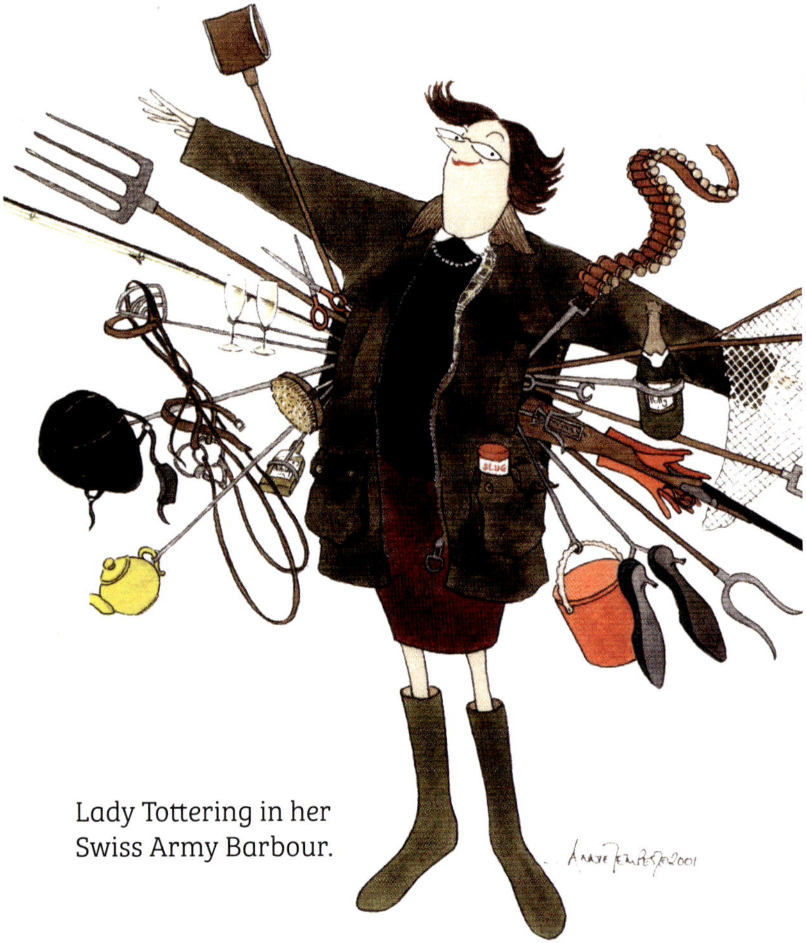
SLUG

Lady Tottering in her Swiss Army Barbour.

joy to the world.

The genius is that each character has its own distinct personality. Dicky and Daffy may be blissfully, happily married, but they view the world through very different lenses. I believe it is this relationship of shared interests and passions seen through contrasting male and female perspectives – along with Annie's clever observations of this dynamic – that is at the heart of the enduring success of 'Tottering-by-Gently'.

This book, which has been ingeniously curated by Raymond O'Shea, brings together the best of shooting, hunting, fishing, horses and Pony Club exploits, as well as golf, cricket, tennis, rugby, skiing, billiards and sailing.

They are busy people, those Totterings – there's not much they can't turn their hand to, which is why they mean so much to each and every one of us.

Mark Hedges
Editor of Country Life

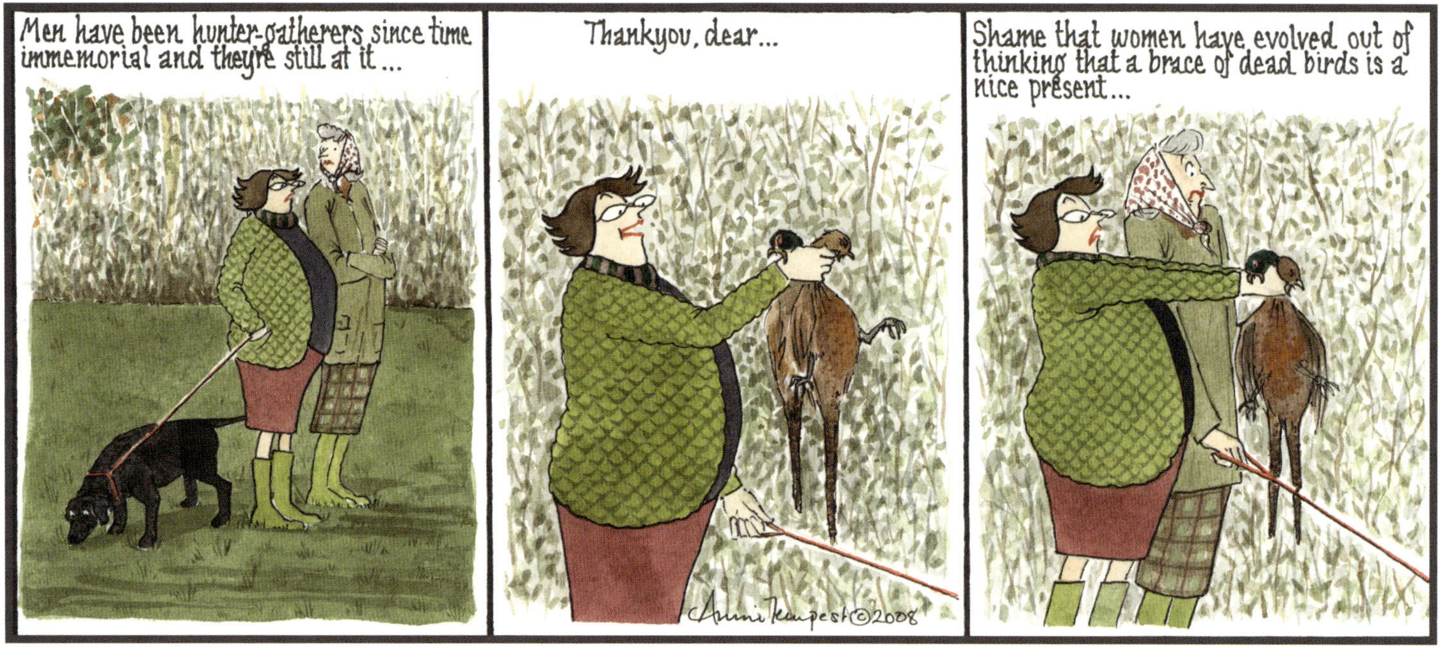
Men have been hunter-gatherers since time immemorial and they're still at it ...
Thankyou, dear...
Anni Tempest ©2008
Shame that women have evolved out of thinking that a brace of dead birds is a nice present...

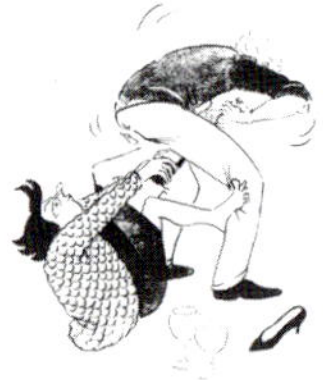

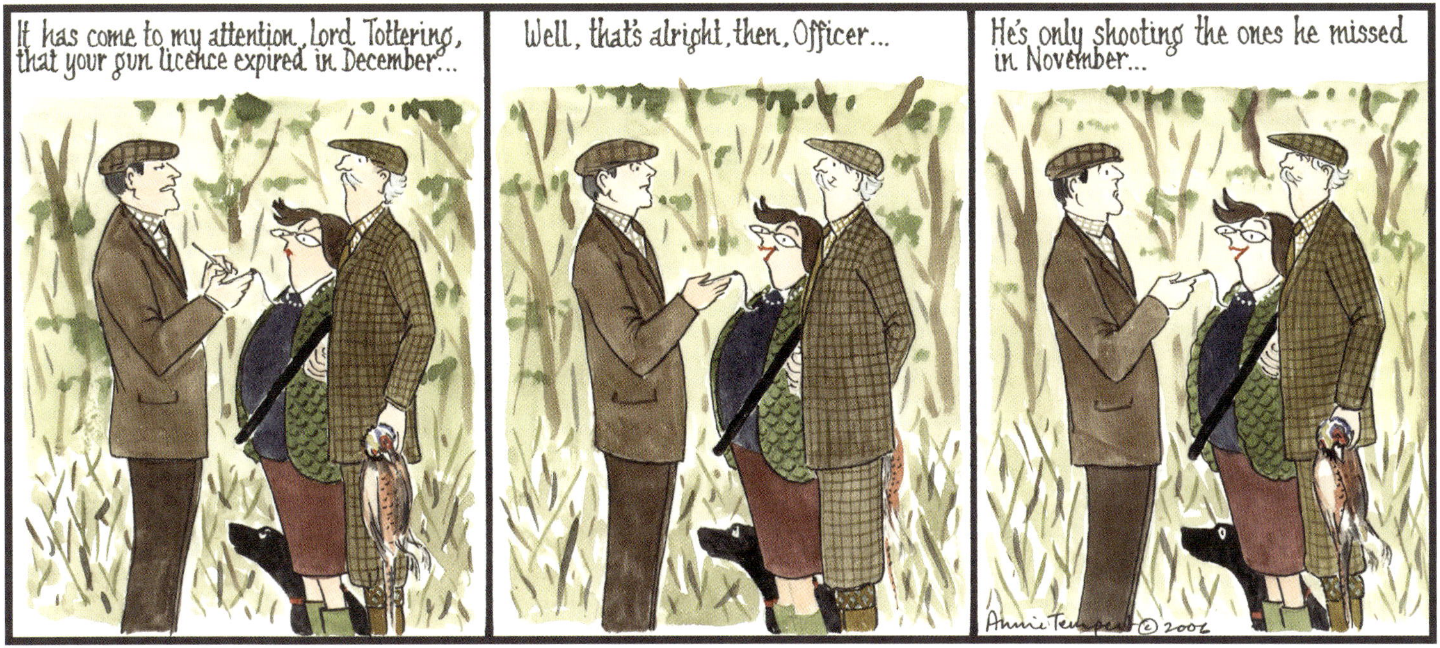

It has come to my attention, Lord Tottering, that your gun licence expired in December...
Well, that's alright, then, Officer...
He's only shooting the ones he missed in November...
Annie Tempest © 2006

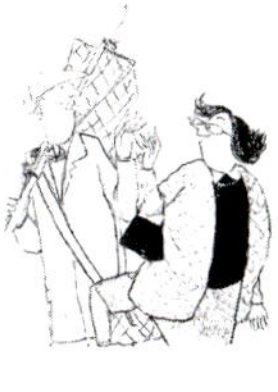

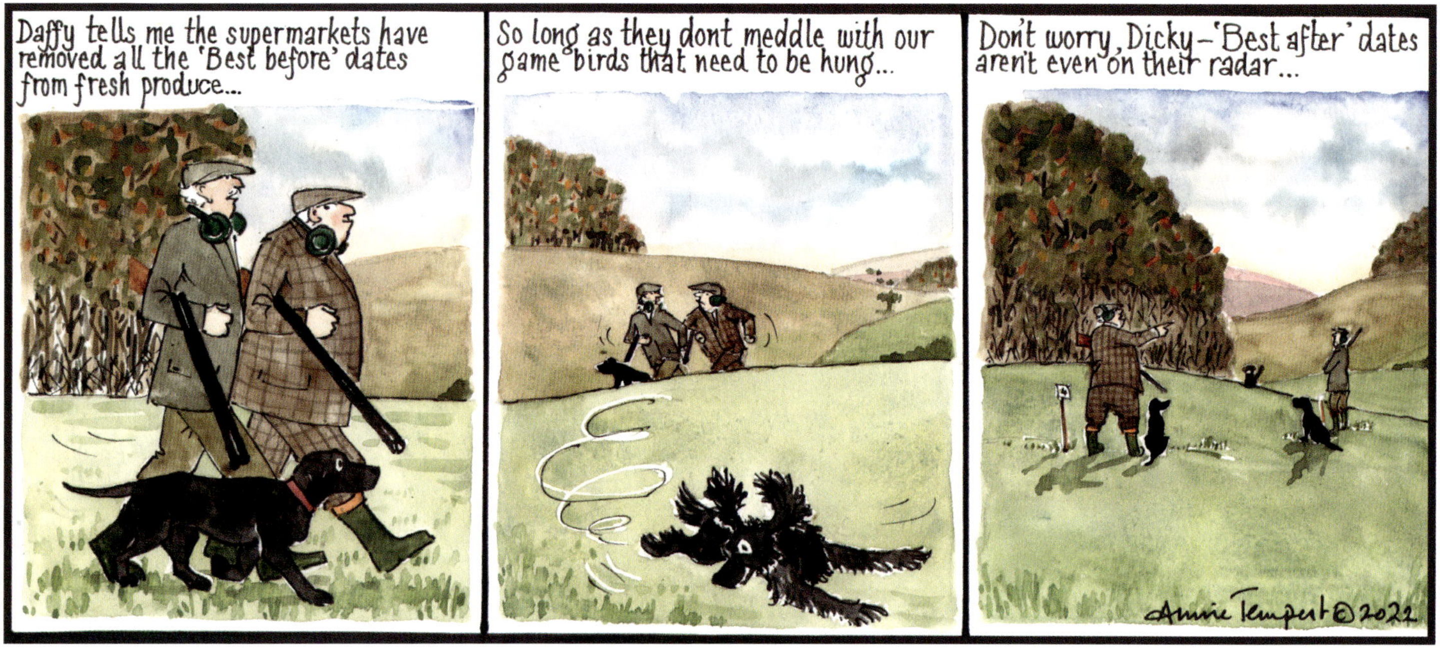
Daffy tells me the supermarkets have removed all the 'Best before' dates from fresh produce...
So long as they dont meddle with our game birds that need to be hung...
Don't worry, Dicky – 'Best after' dates aren't even on their radar...
Annie Tempest © 2022

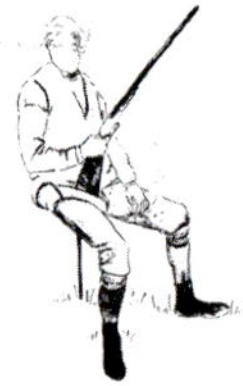

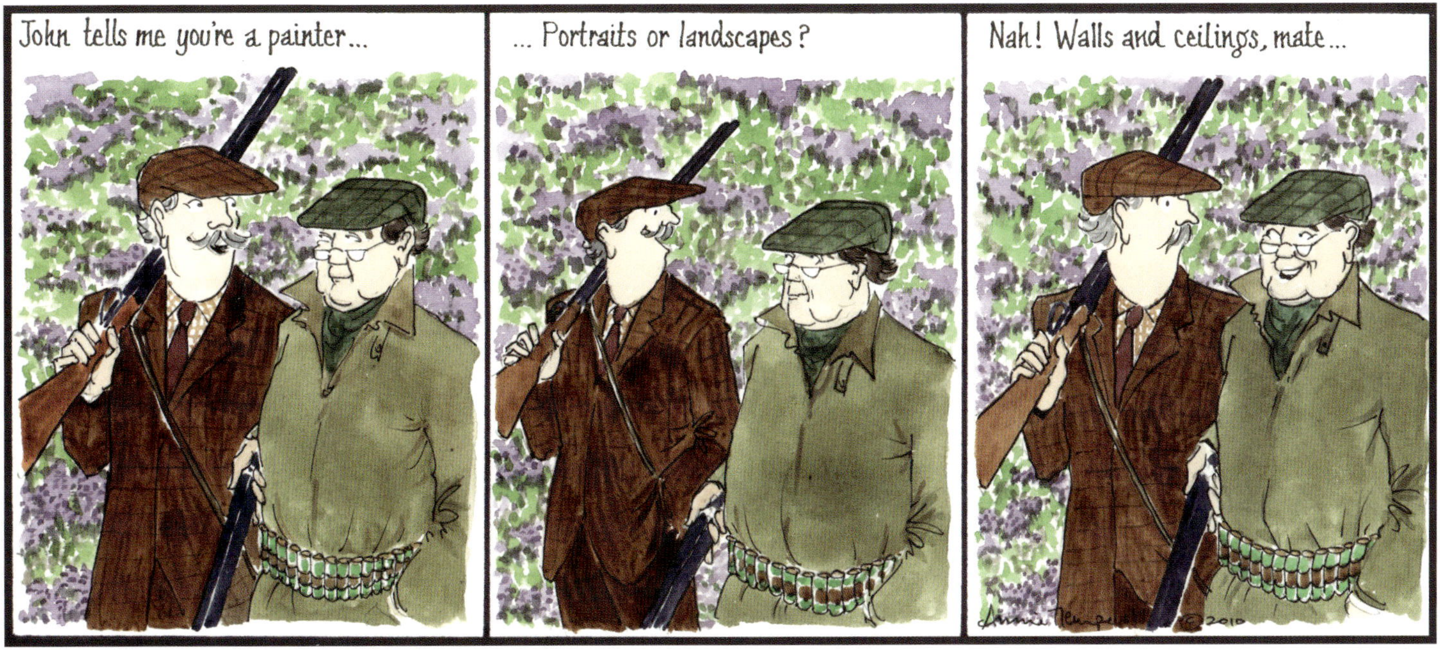
John tells me you're a painter...
... Portraits or landscapes?
Nah! Walls and ceilings, mate...

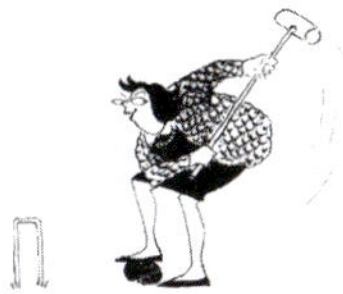

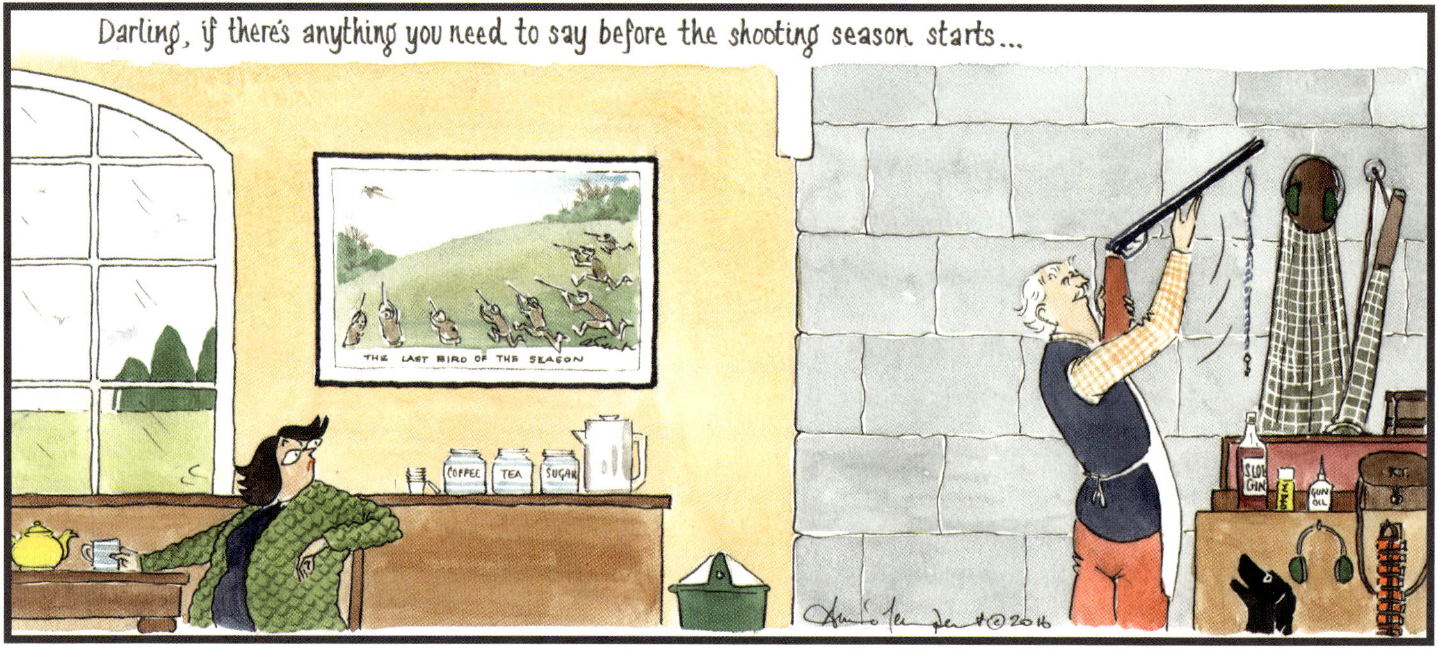
THE LAST BIRD OF THE SEASON
COFFEE
TEA
SUGAR
SLOE GIN
GUN OIL
Darling, if there's anything you need to say before the shooting season starts...

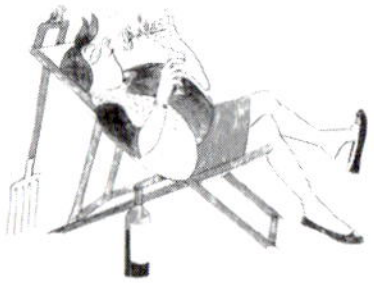

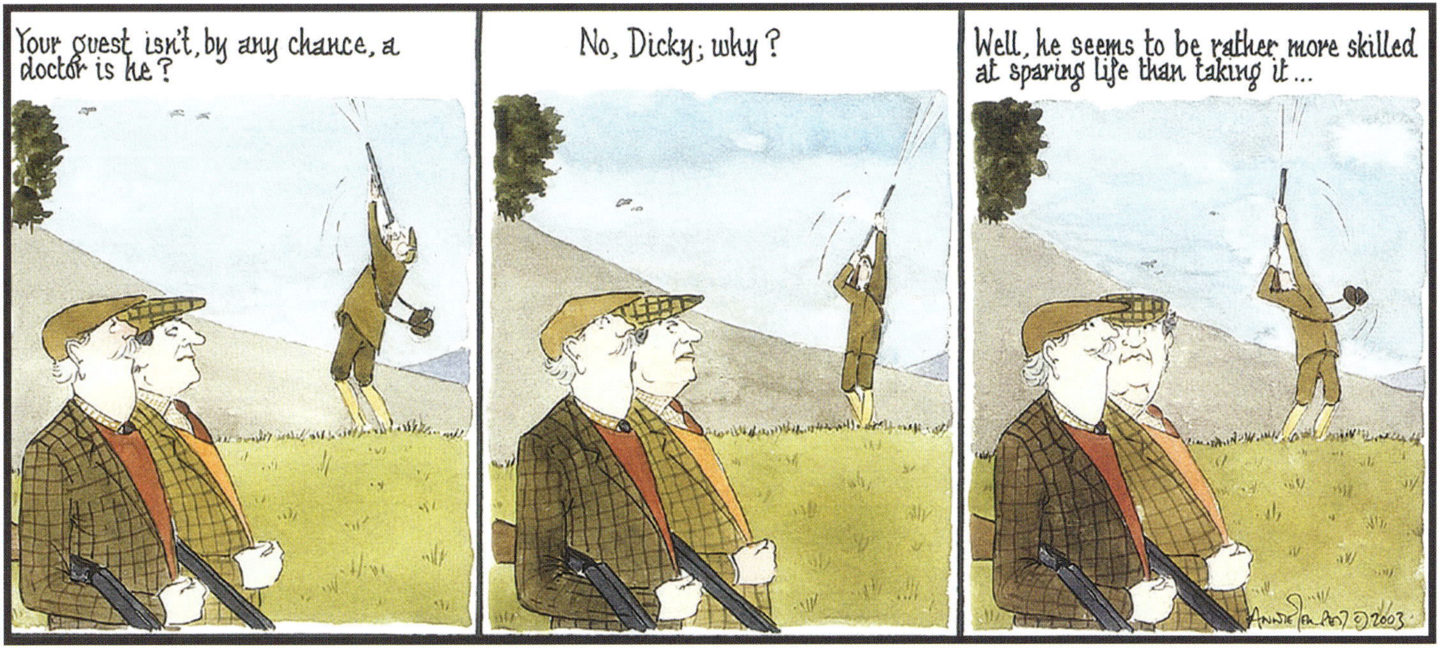
Your guest isn't, by any chance, a doctor is he?
No, Dicky; why?
Well, he seems to be rather more skilled at sparing life than taking it...
ANNIE TEMPEST ©2003

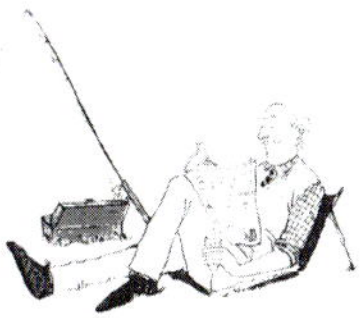

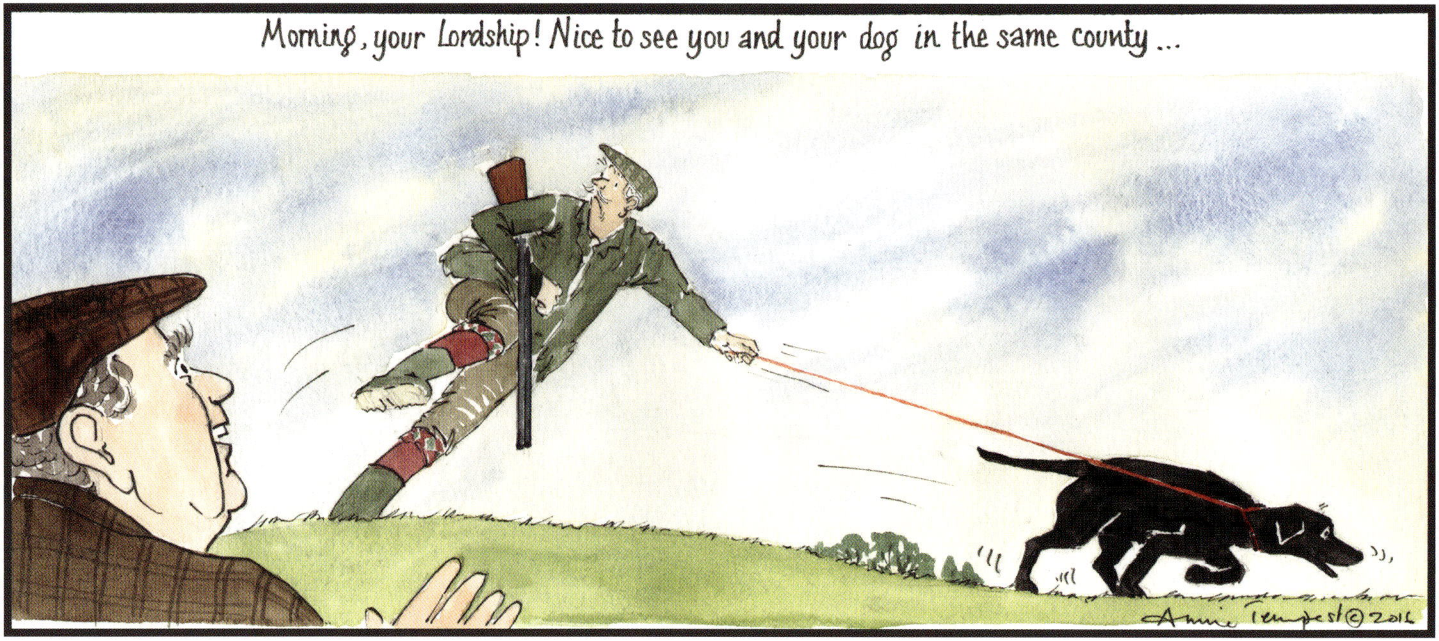
Morning, your Lordship! Nice to see you and your dog in the same county ...

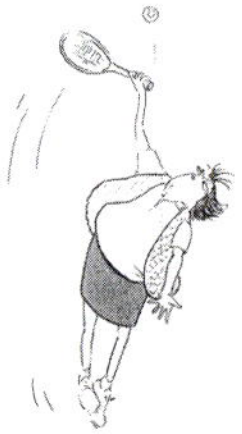

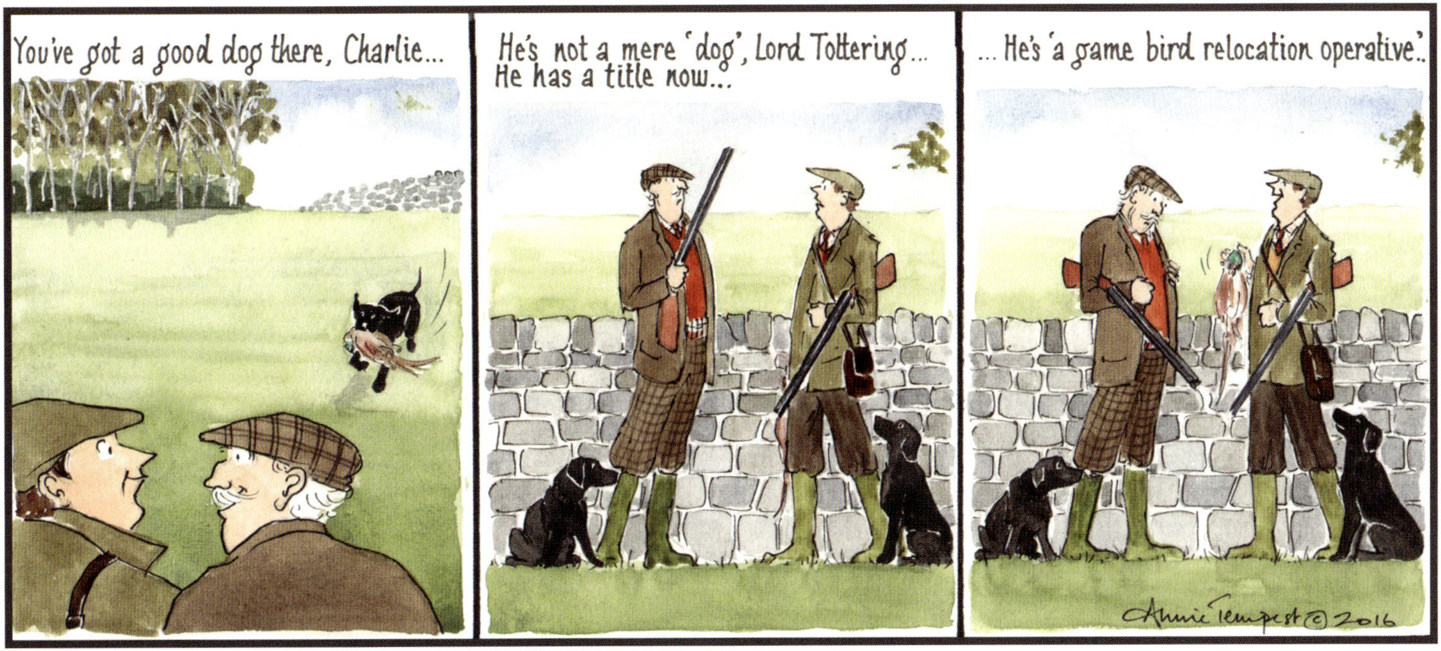
You've got a good dog there, Charlie...
He's not a mere 'dog', Lord Tottering...
He has a title now...
... He's 'a game bird relocation operative'.
Annie Tempest © 2016

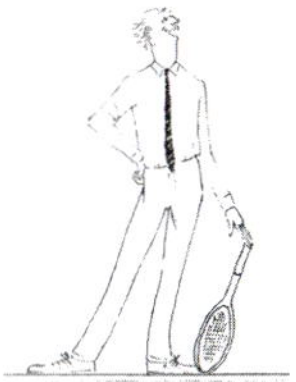

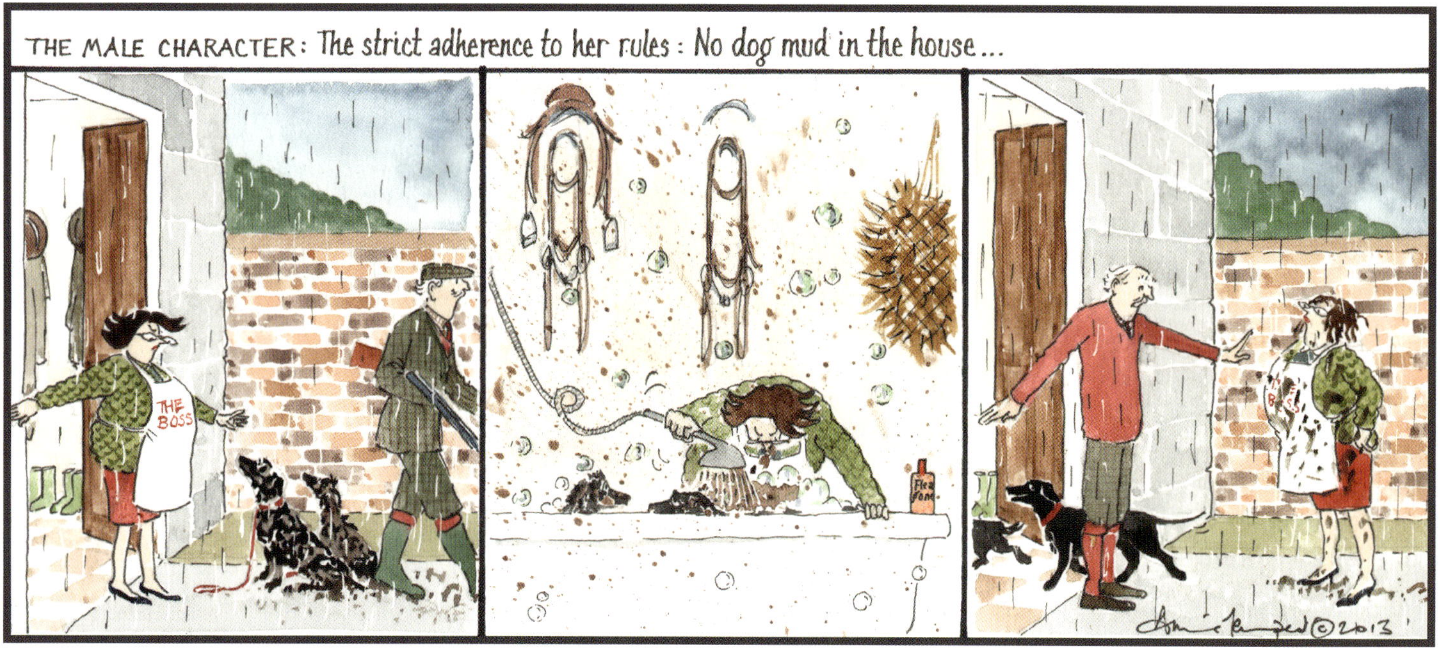
THE MALE CHARACTER: The strict adherence to her rules: No dog mud in the house...
THE BOSS

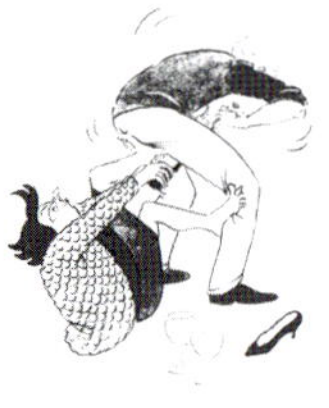

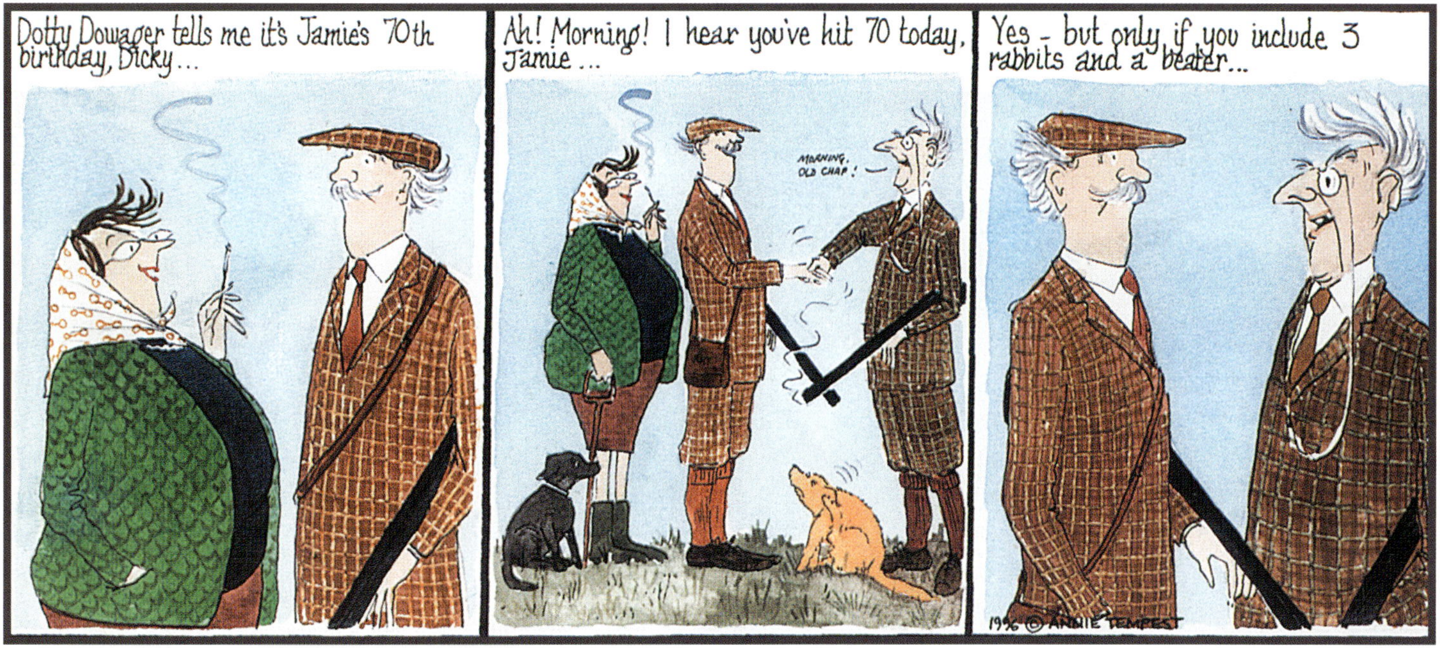
Dotty Dowager tells me it's Jamie's 70th birthday, Dicky...
Ah! Morning! I hear you've hit 70 today, Jamie...
MORNING, OLD CHAP!
Yes - but only if you include 3 rabbits and a beater...
1996 © ANNIE TEMPEST

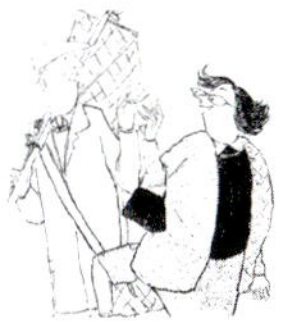

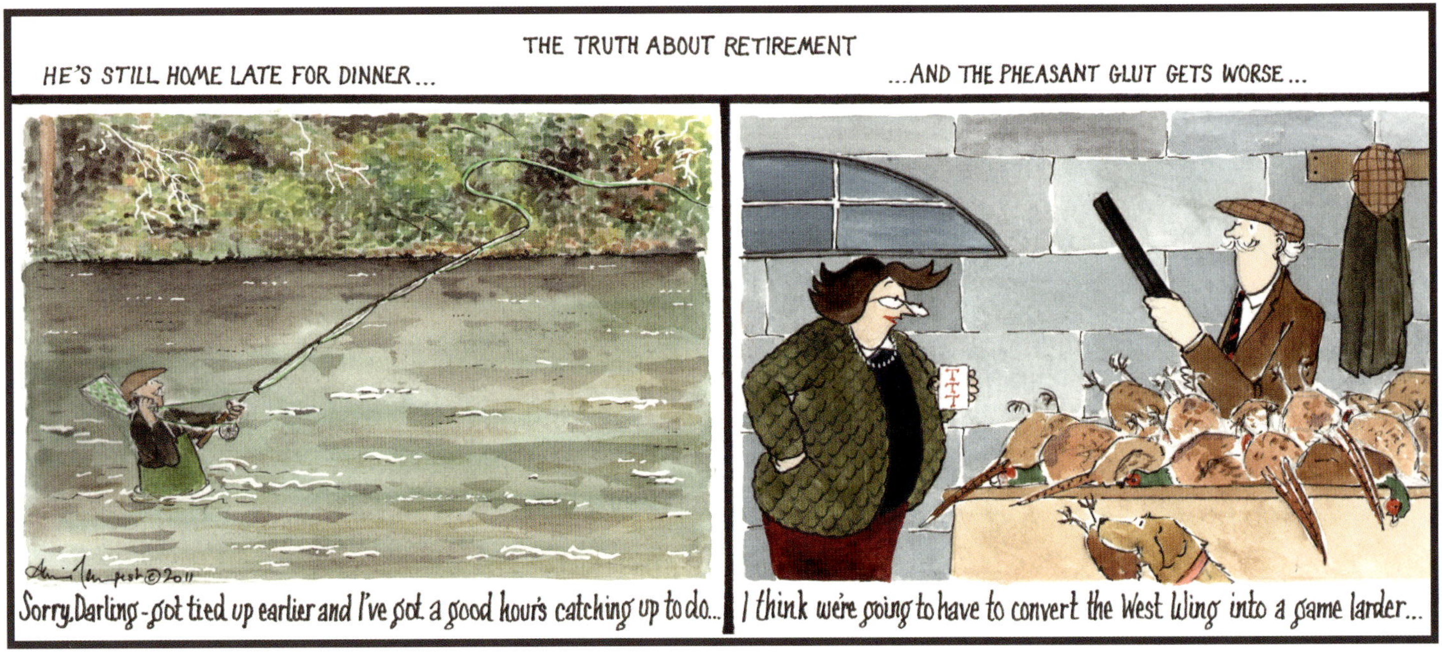
THE TRUTH ABOUT RETIREMENT
HE'S STILL HOME LATE FOR DINNER...
...AND THE PHEASANT GLUT GETS WORSE...
Sorry, Darling - got tied up earlier and I've got a good hour's catching up to do...
I think we're going to have to convert the West Wing into a game larder...

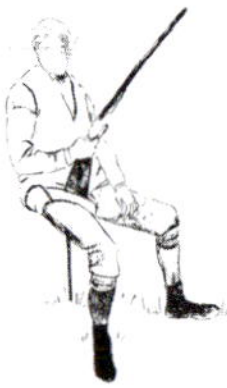

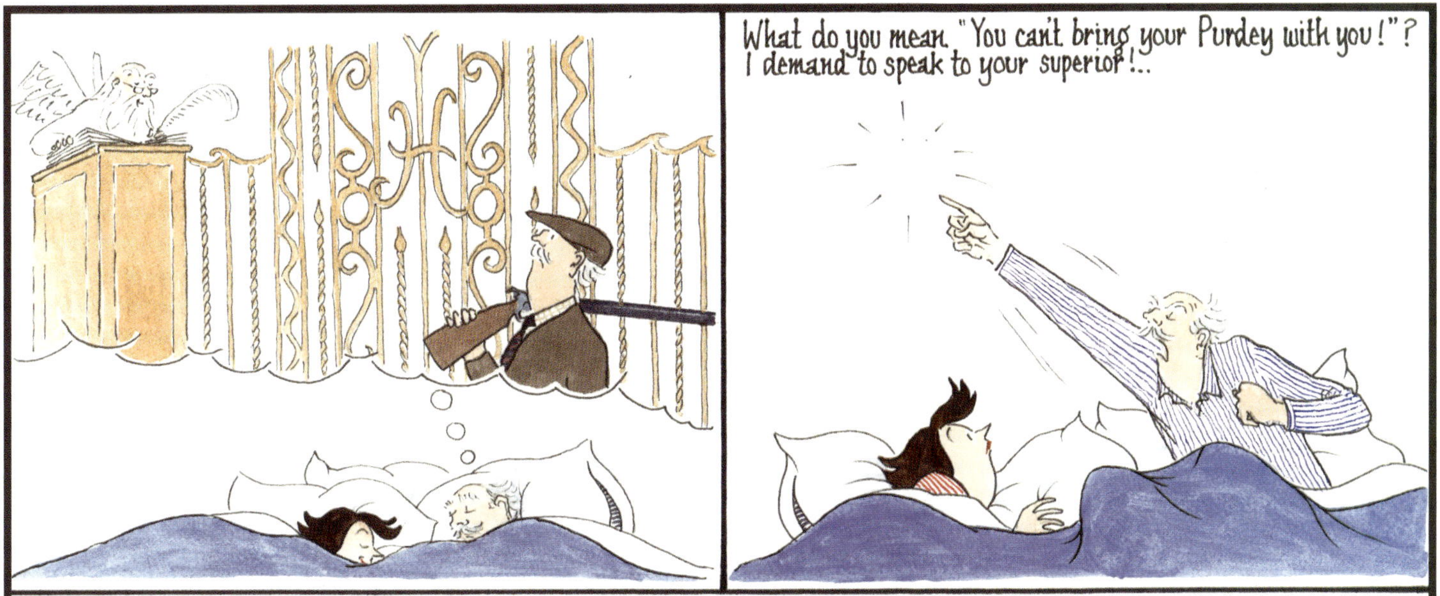
What do you mean "You can't bring your Purdey with you!"?
I demand to speak to your superior!...

THE GUN'S NIGHTMARE...

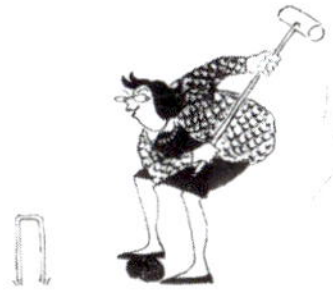

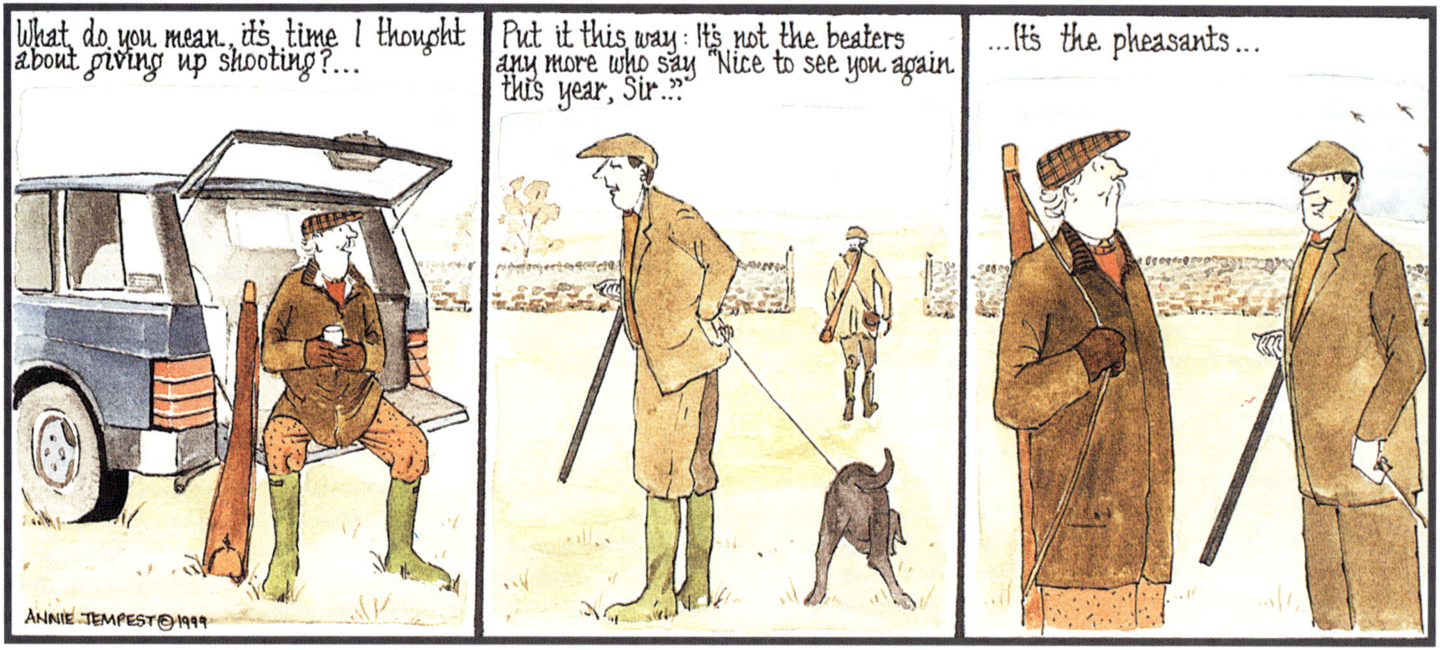
What do you mean, it's time I thought about giving up shooting?...
ANNIE TEMPEST © 1999
Put it this way: It's not the beaters any more who say "Nice to see you again this year, Sir..."
...It's the pheasants...

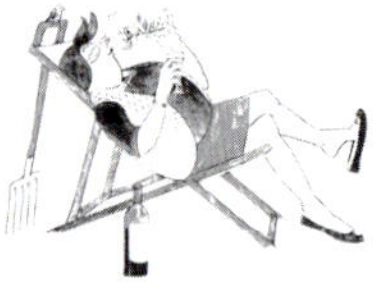

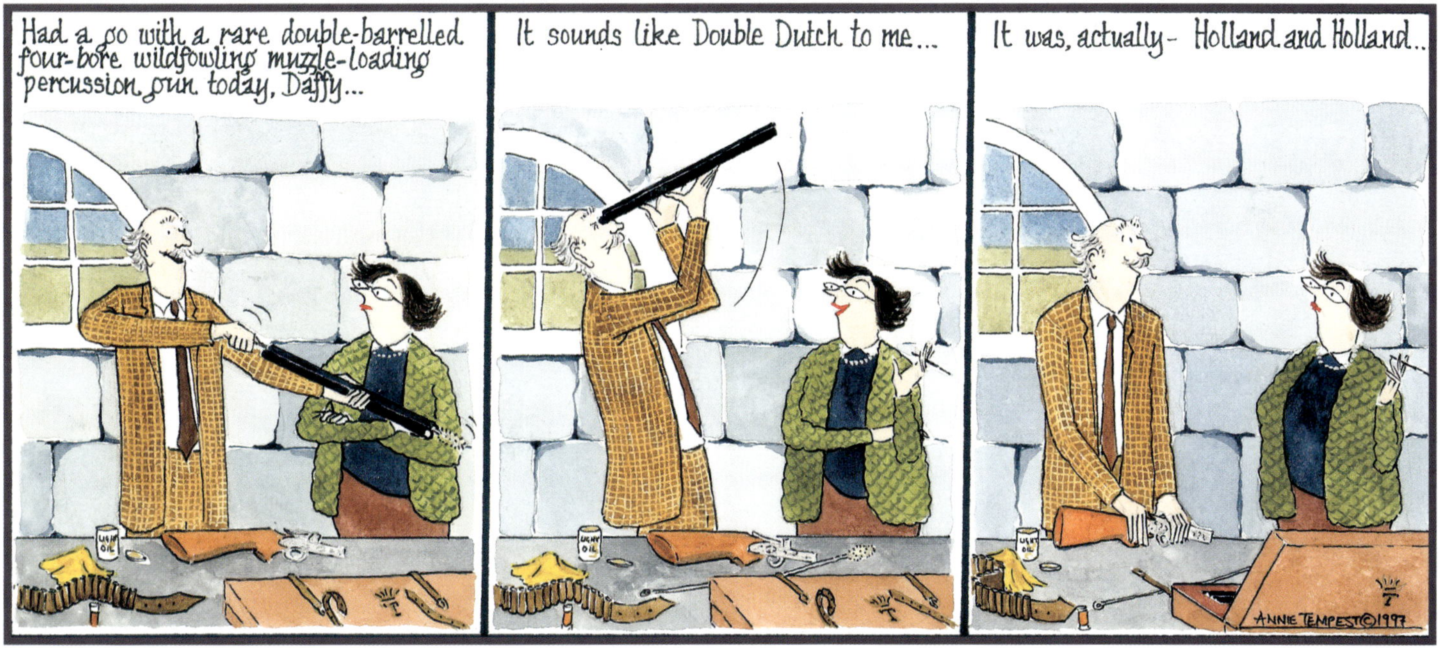
Had a go with a rare double-barrelled four-bore wildfowling muzzle-loading percussion gun today, Daffy...
It sounds like Double Dutch to me...
It was, actually - Holland and Holland...
ANNIE TEMPEST©1997

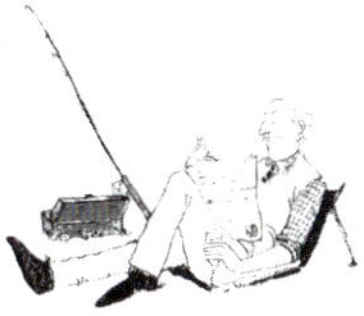

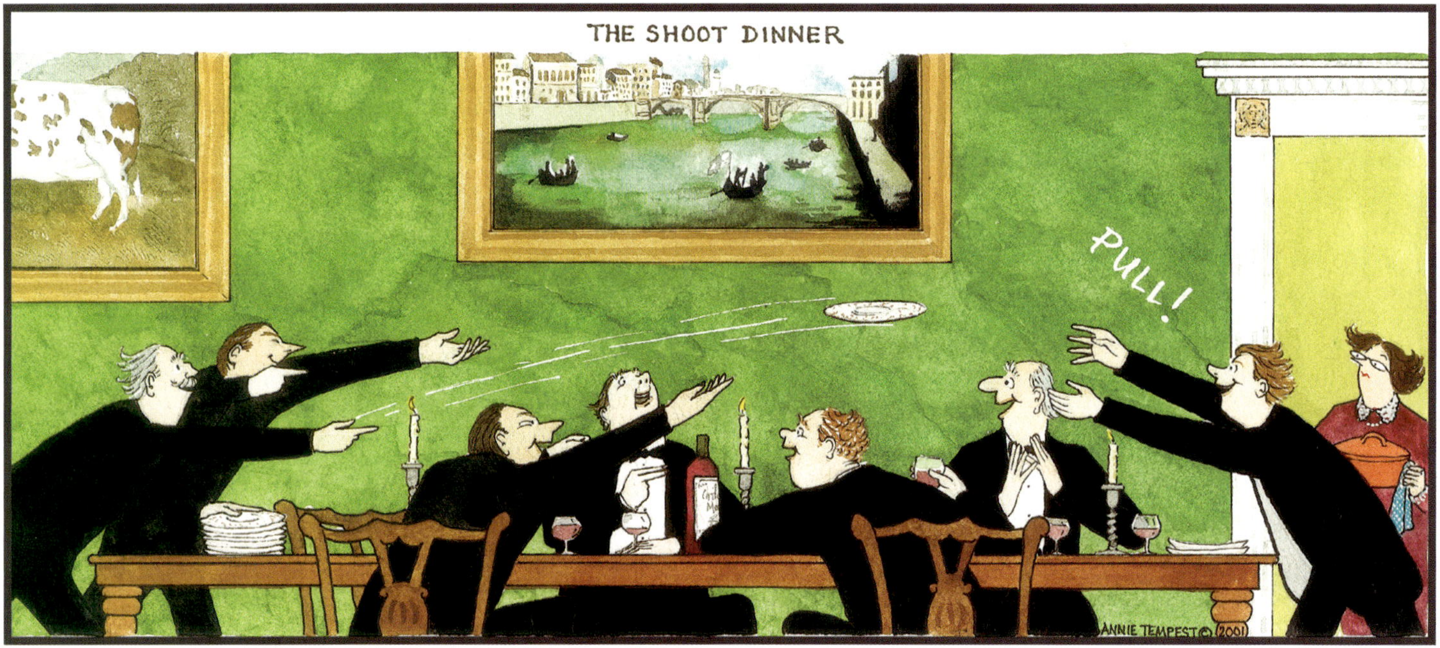
THE SHOOT DINNER
PULL!
ANNIE TEMPEST © 2001

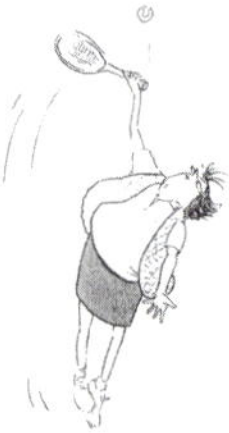

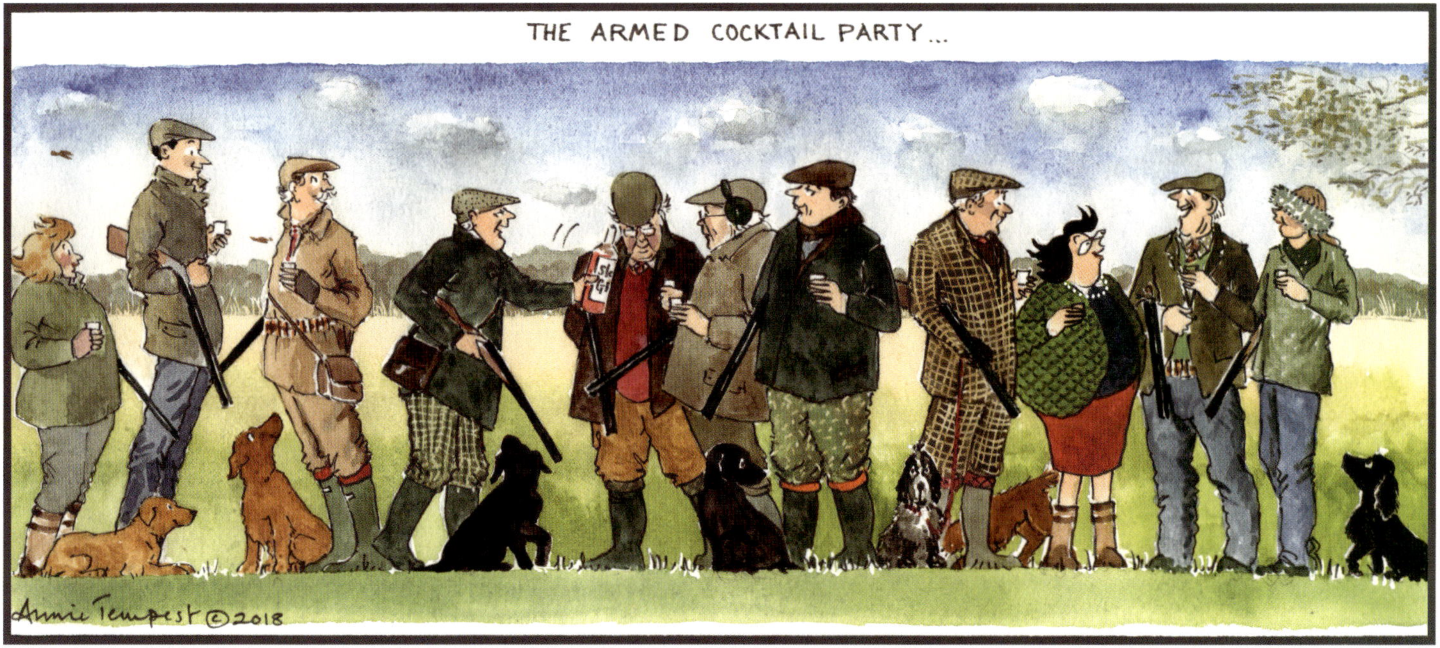
THE ARMED COCKTAIL PARTY...
Annie Tempest ©2018

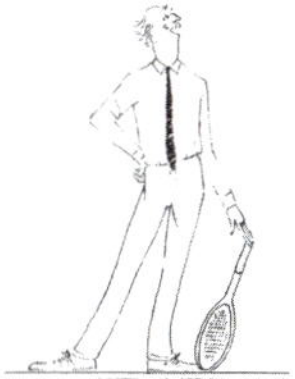

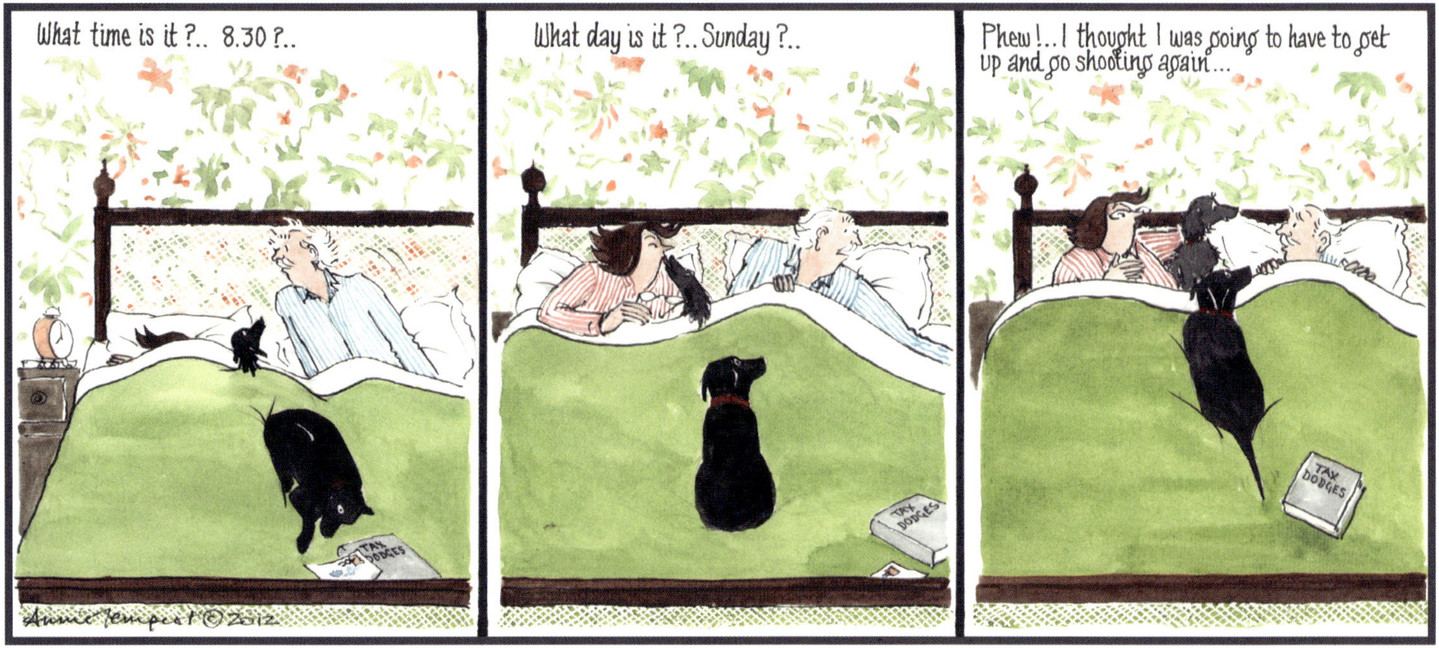
What time is it ?.. 8.30 ?..
TAX DODGES
Annie Tempest © 2012
What day is it ?.. Sunday ?..
TAX DODGES
Phew !.. I thought I was going to have to get up and go shooting again...
TAX DODGES

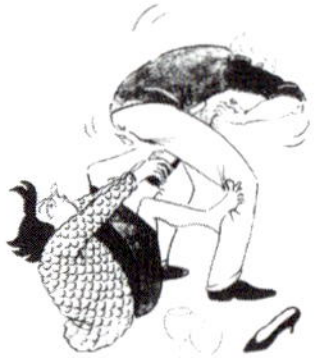

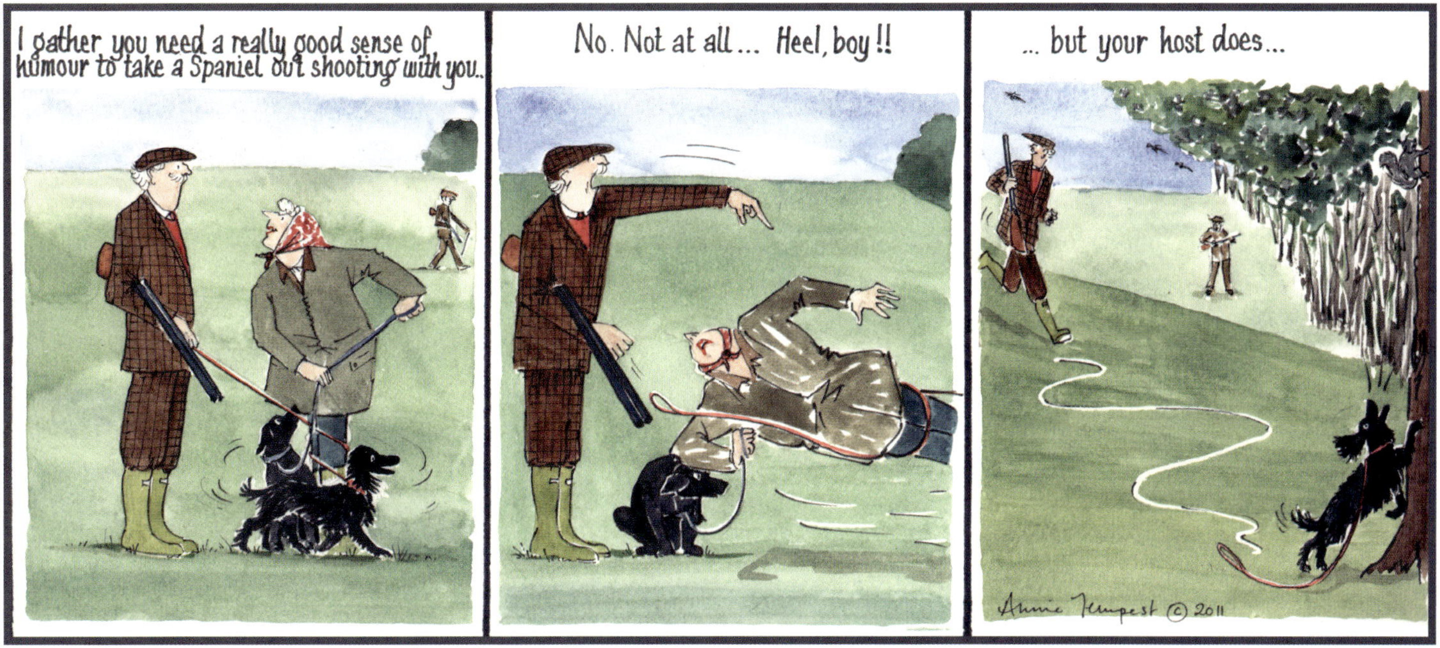
I gather you need a really good sense of humour to take a Spaniel out shooting with you..
No. Not at all... Heel, boy!!
... but your host does...
Annie Tempest © 2011

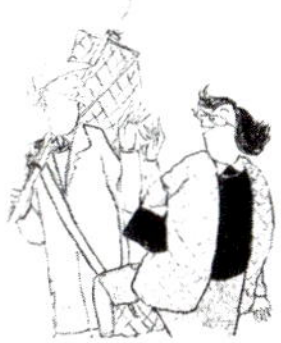

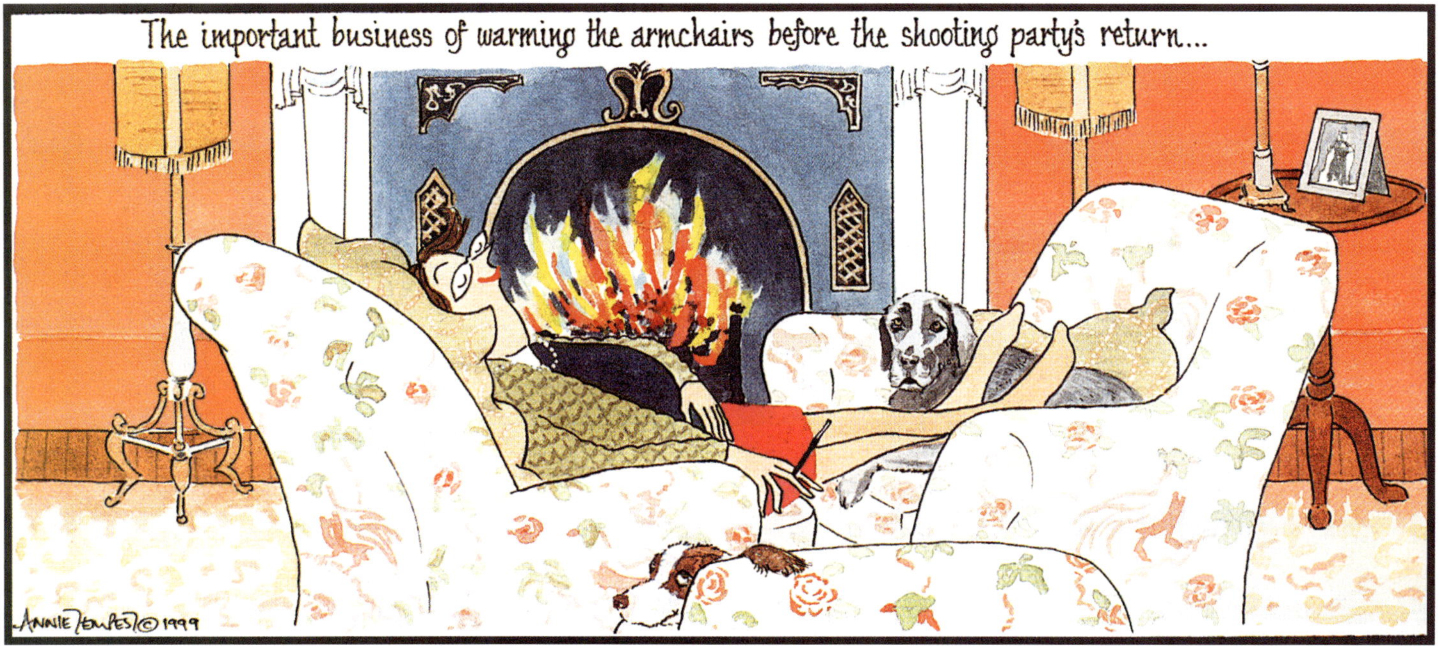
ANNIE TEMPEST © 1999

The important business of warming the armchairs before the shooting party's return...

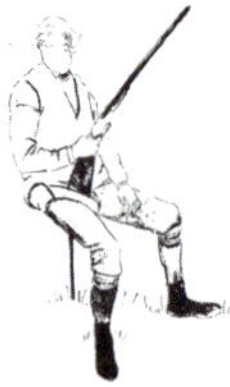

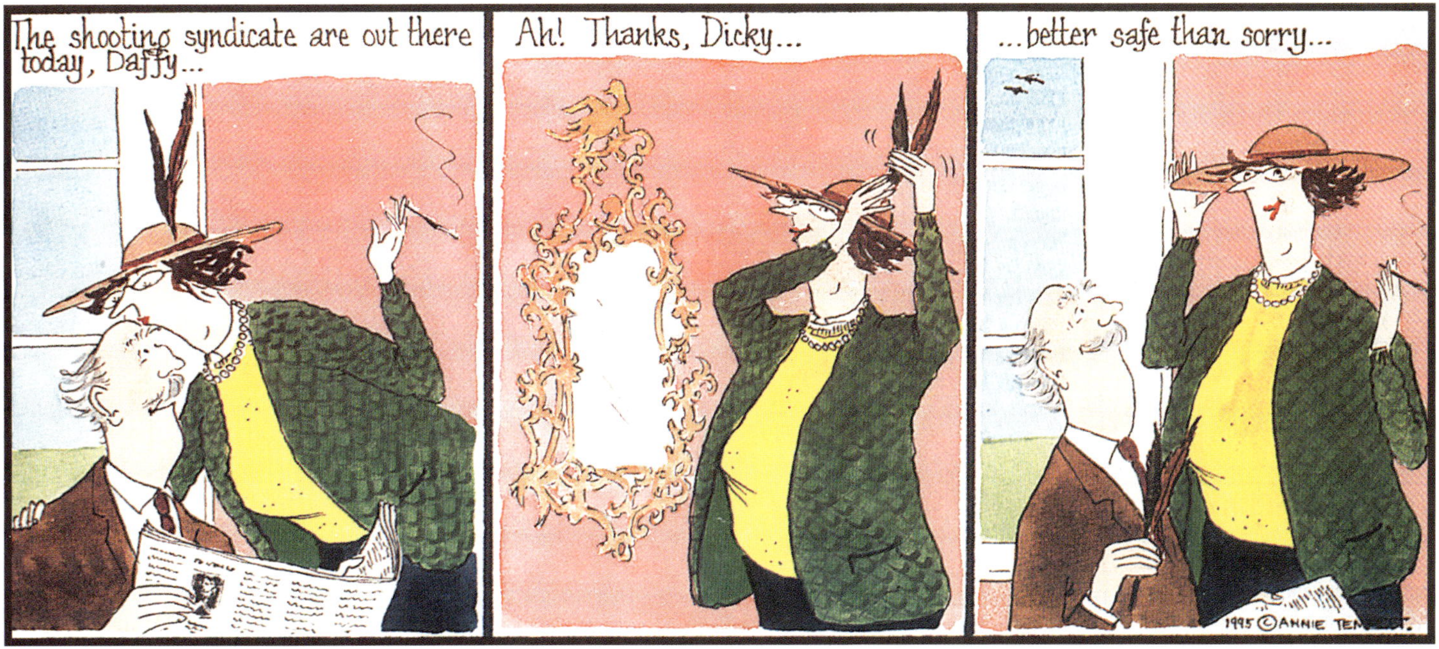
The shooting syndicate are out there today, Daffy…
Ah! Thanks, Dicky…
…better safe than sorry…
1995 ©ANNIE TEN

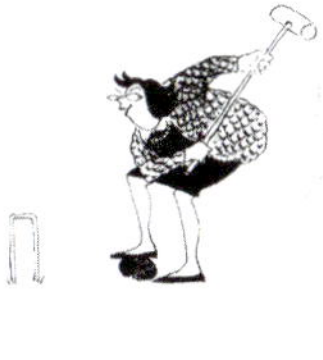

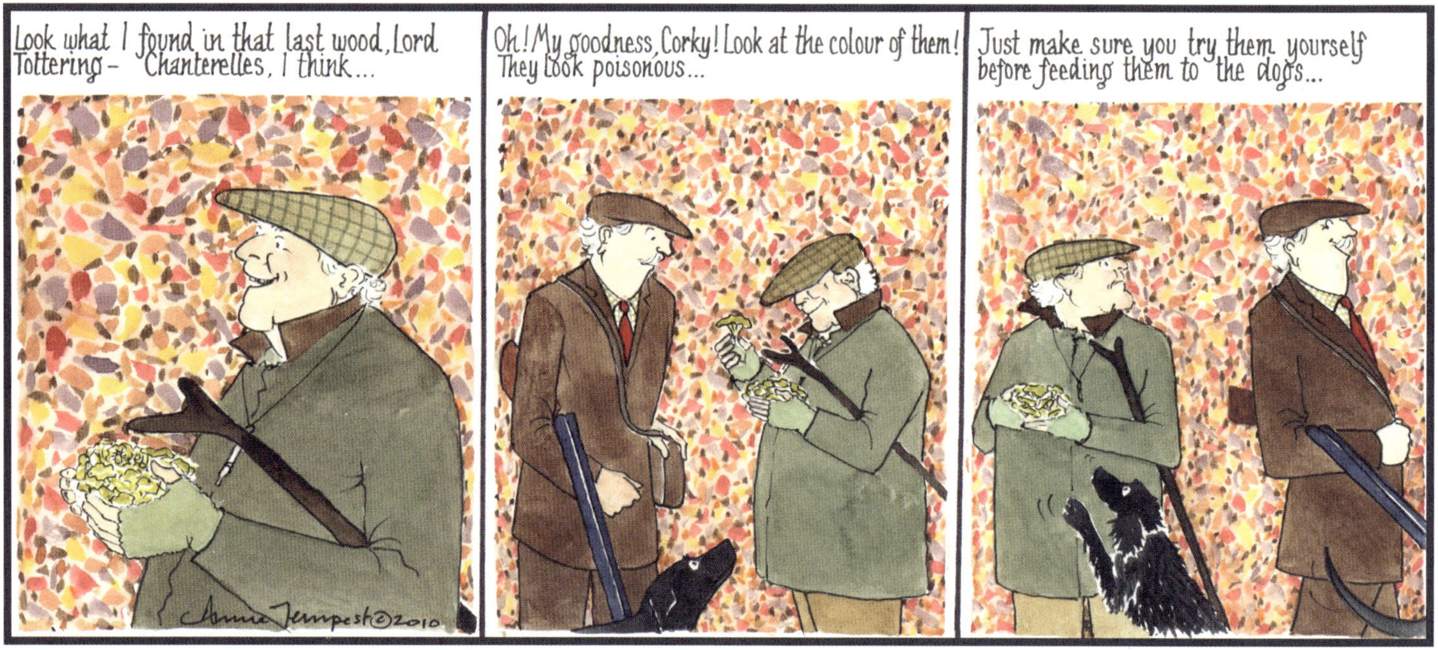
Look what I found in that last wood, Lord Tottering - Chanterelles, I think...
Oh! My goodness, Corky! Look at the colour of them! They look poisonous...
Just make sure you try them yourself before feeding them to the dogs...
Annie Tempest©2010

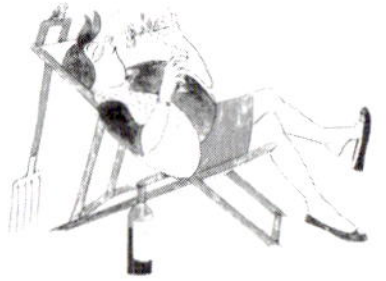

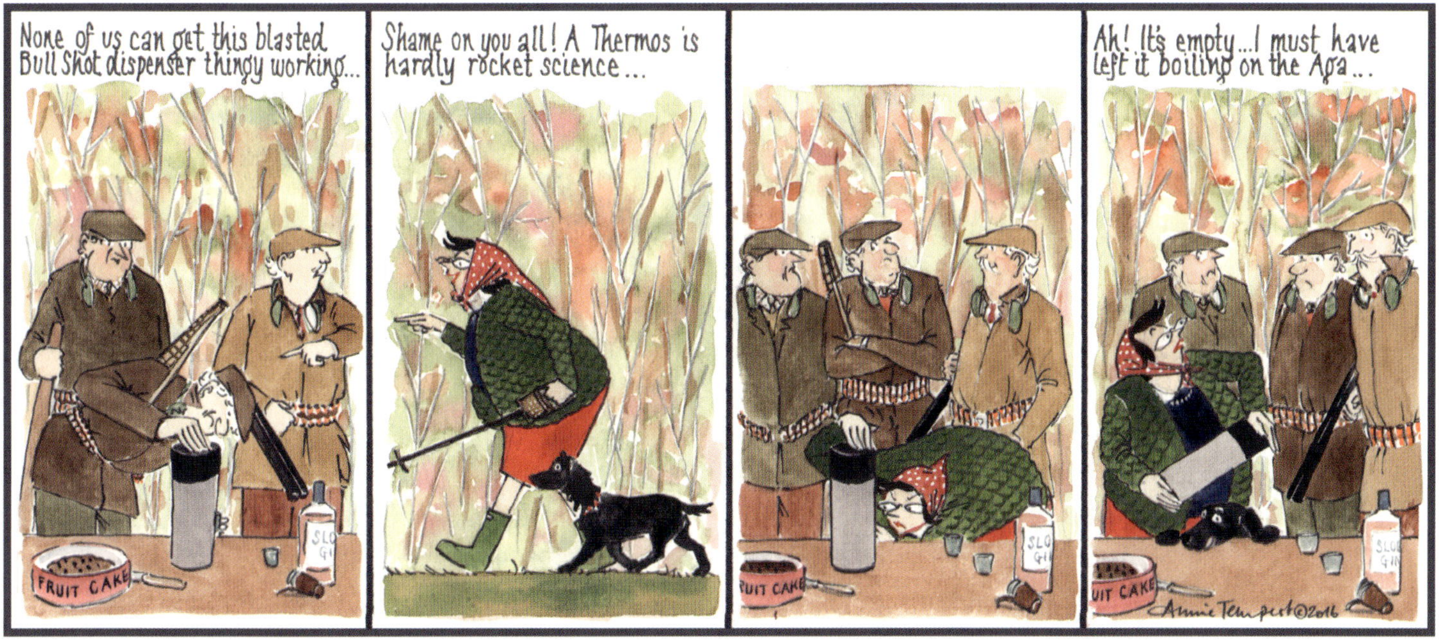
None of us can get this blasted Bull Shot dispenser thingy working...
FRUIT CAKE
Shame on you all! A Thermos is hardly rocket science...
Ah! It's empty...I must have left it boiling on the Aga...
Annie Tempest ©2016

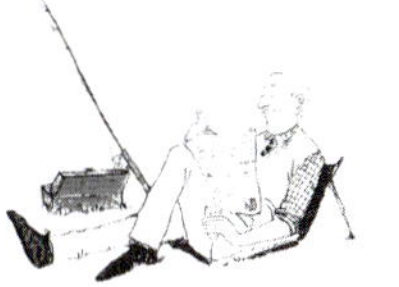

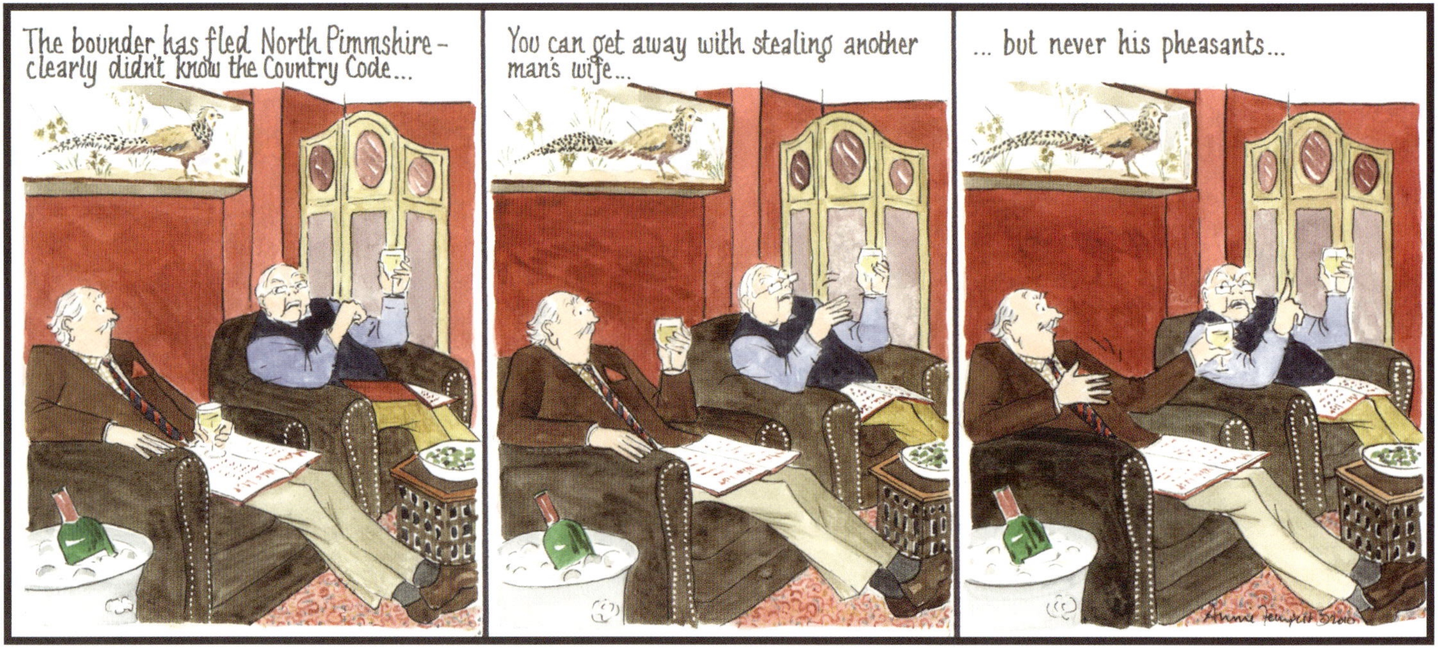
The bounder has fled North Pimmshire - clearly didn't know the Country Code...
You can get away with stealing another man's wife...
... but never his pheasants...

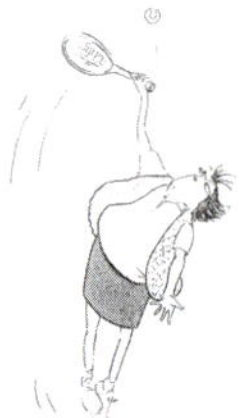

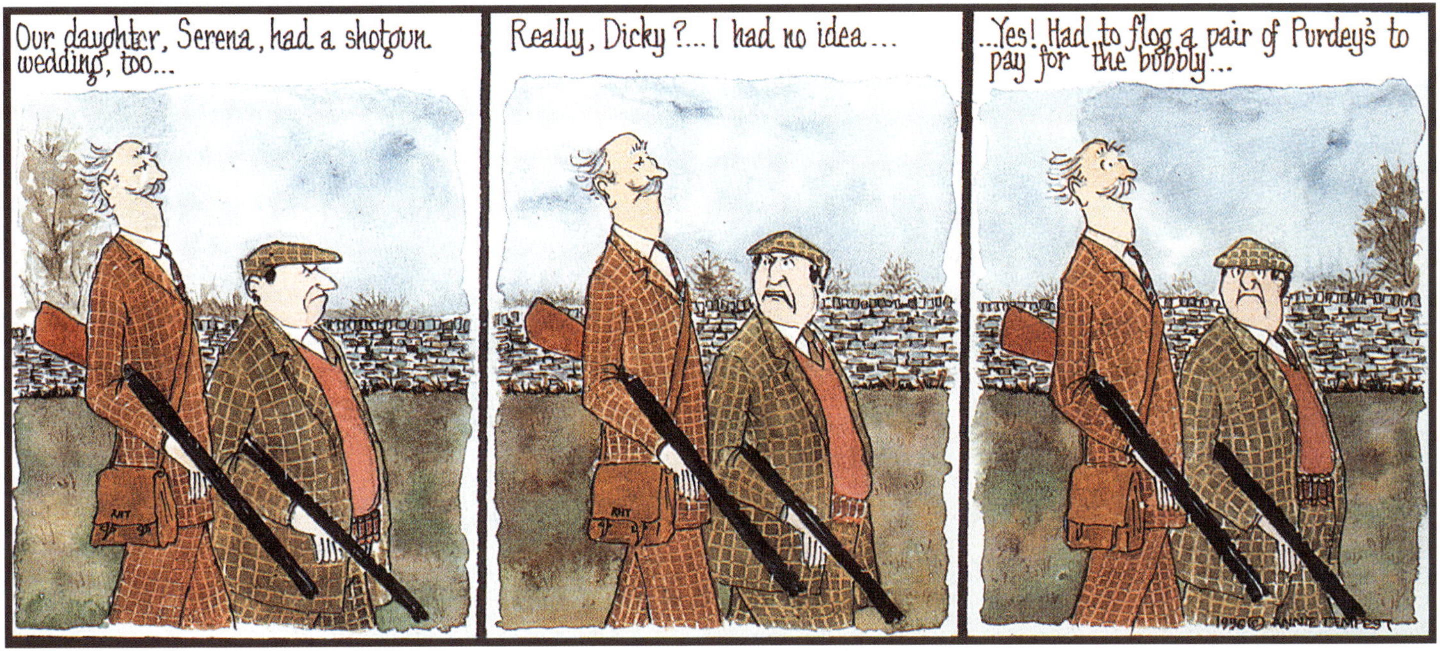
Our daughter, Serena, had a shotgun wedding, too...
Really, Dicky?... I had no idea...
...Yes! Had to flog a pair of Purdey's to pay for the bubbly!...
1996 © ANNIE TEMPEST

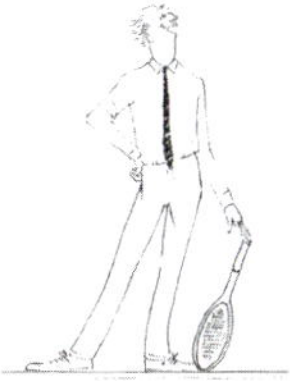

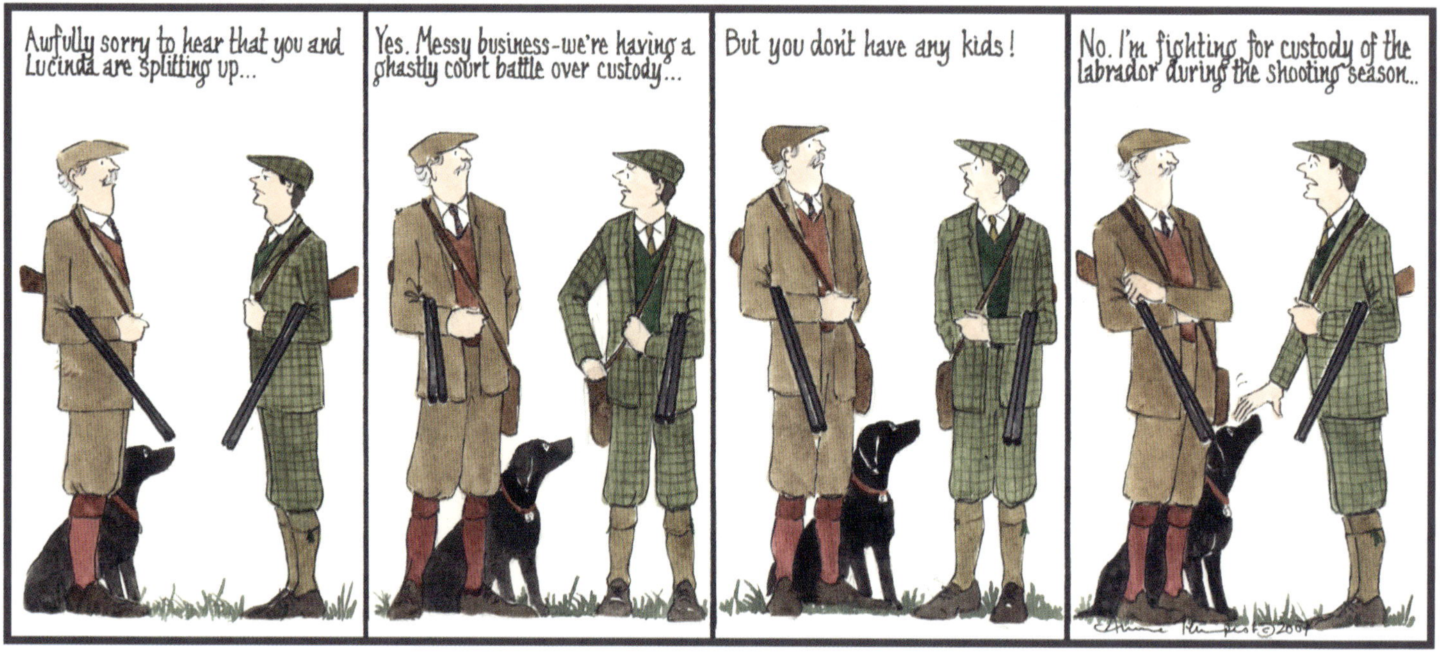
Awfully sorry to hear that you and Lucinda are splitting up...
Yes. Messy business-we're having a ghastly court battle over custody...
But you don't have any kids!
No. I'm fighting for custody of the labrador during the shooting season...

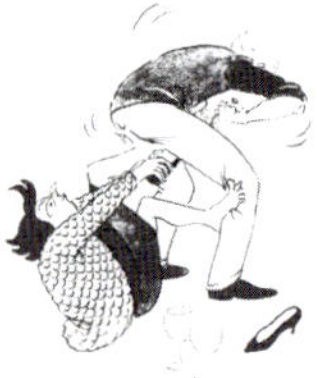

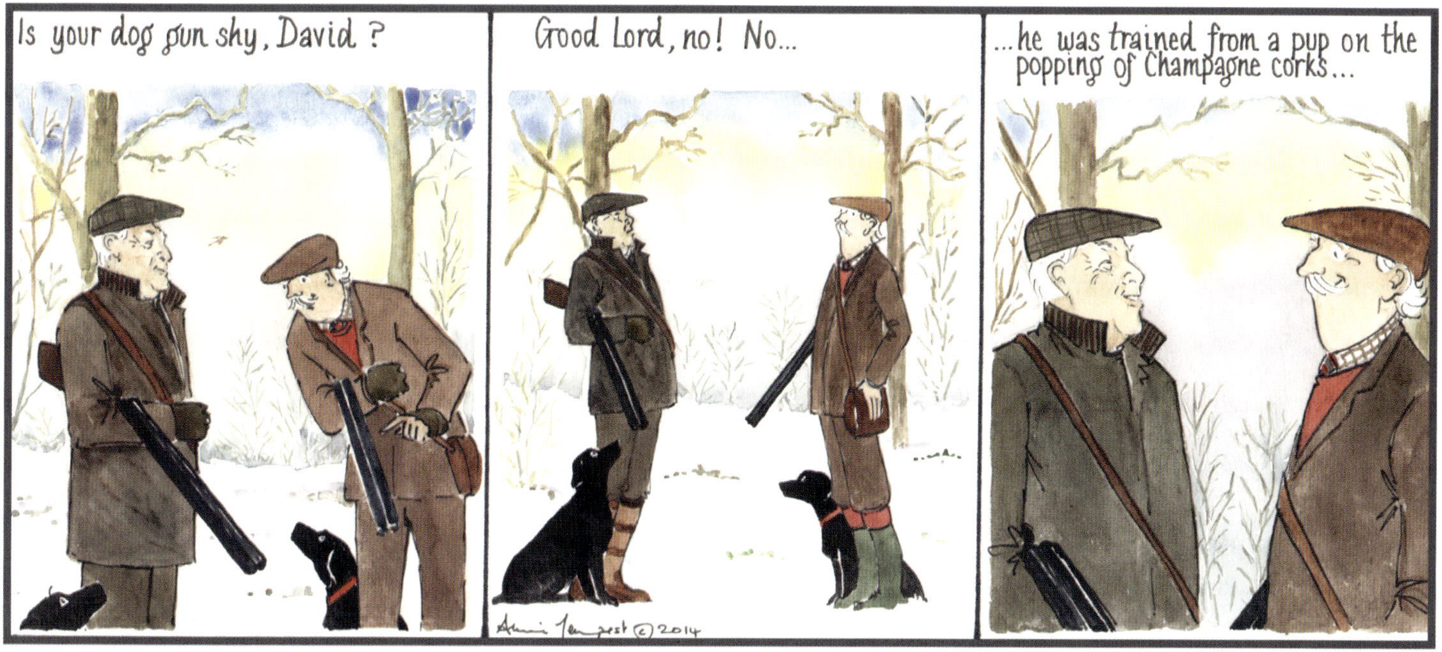
Is your dog gun shy, David?
Good Lord, no! No...
...he was trained from a pup on the popping of Champagne corks...

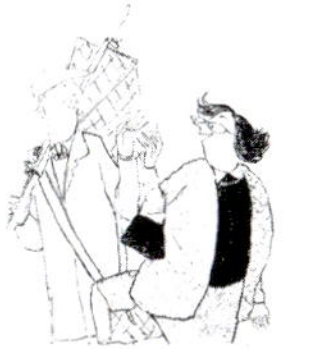

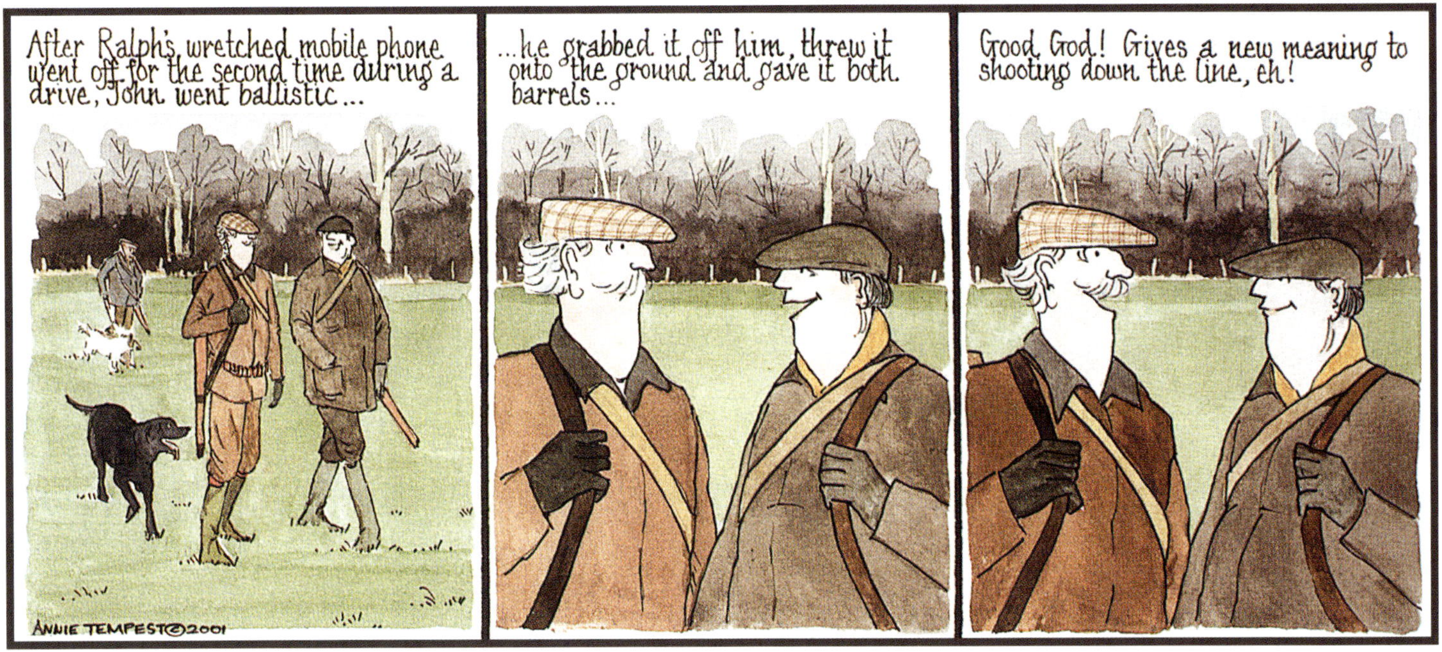
After Ralph's wretched mobile phone went off for the second time during a drive, John went ballistic...
ANNIE TEMPEST©2001
...he grabbed it off him, threw it onto the ground and gave it both barrels...
Good God! Gives a new meaning to shooting down the line, eh!

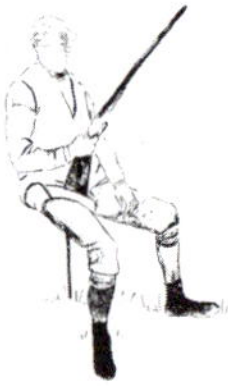

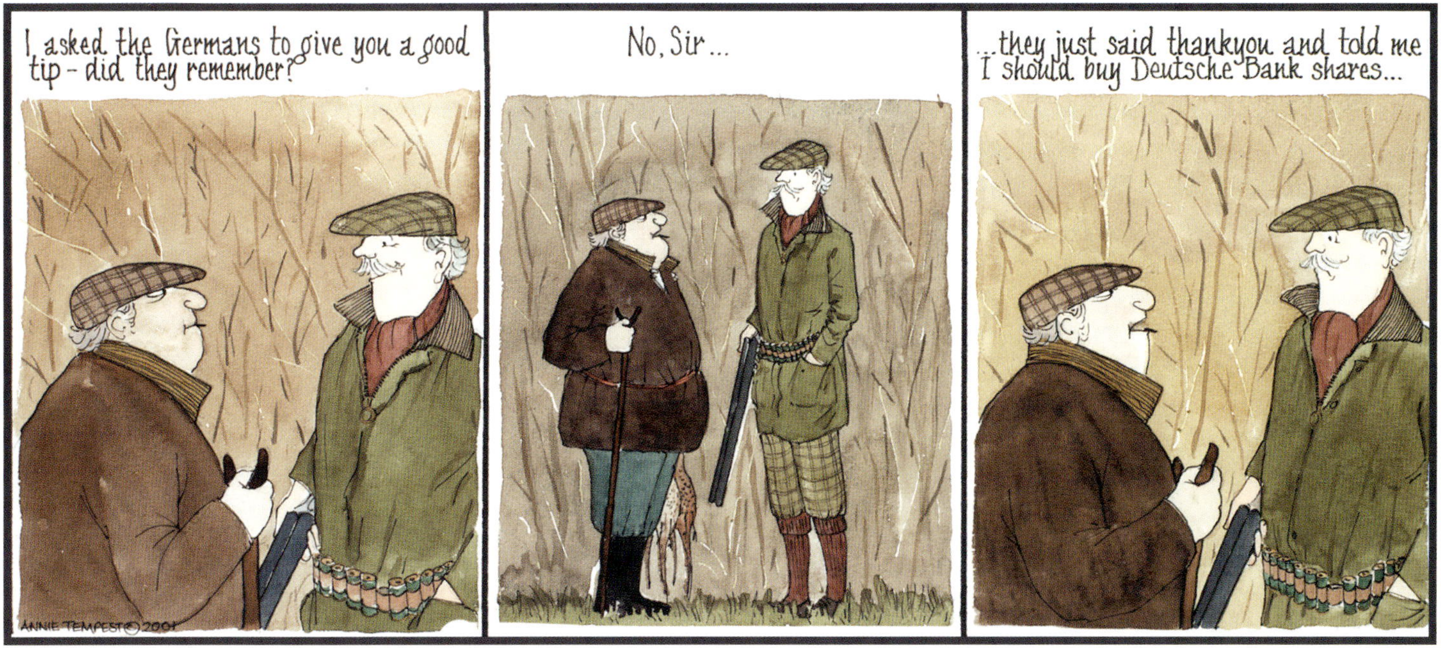
I asked the Germans to give you a good tip - did they remember?
No, Sir...
...they just said thankyou and told me I should buy Deutsche Bank shares...
ANNIE TEMPEST © 2001

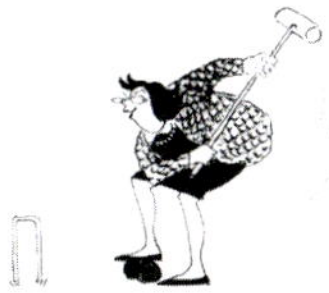

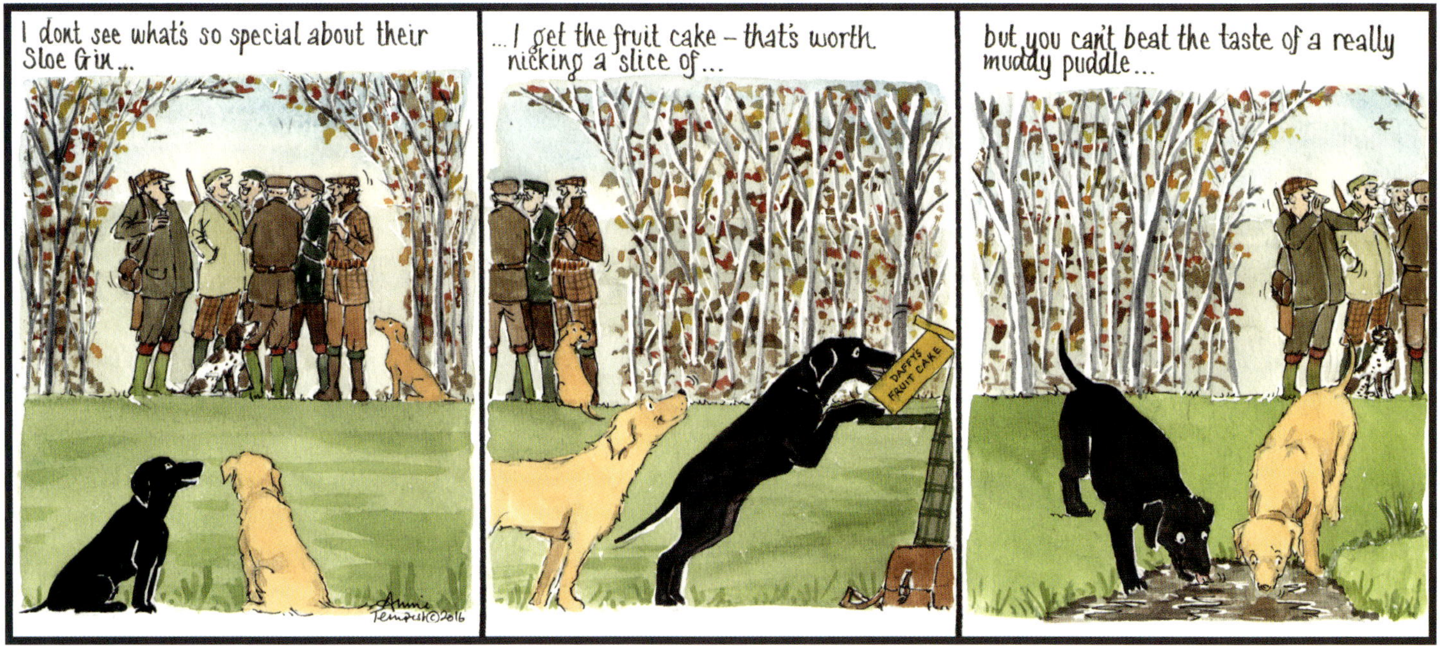
I dont see what's so special about their Sloe Gin...
Annie Tempest©2016
...I get the fruit cake – that's worth nicking a slice of...
DAFFY'S FRUIT CAKE
but you can't beat the taste of a really muddy puddle...

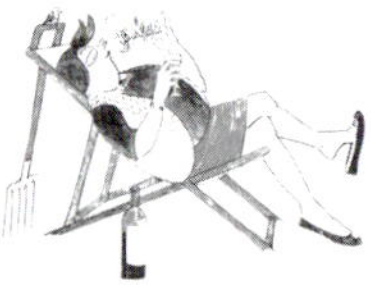

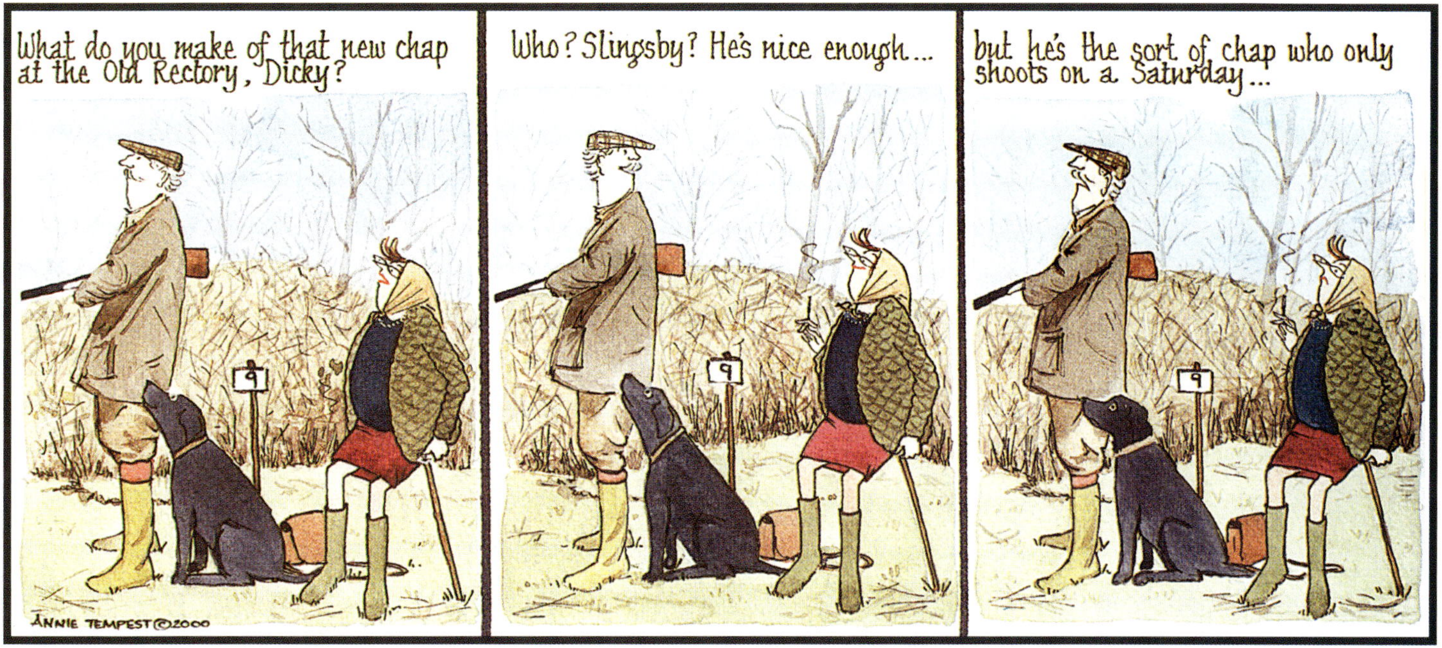
What do you make of that new chap at the Old Rectory, Dicky?
Who? Slingsby? He's nice enough...
but he's the sort of chap who only shoots on a Saturday...
ANNIE TEMPEST ©2000

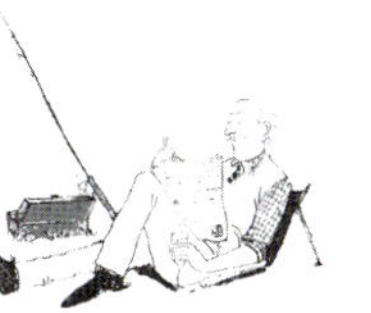

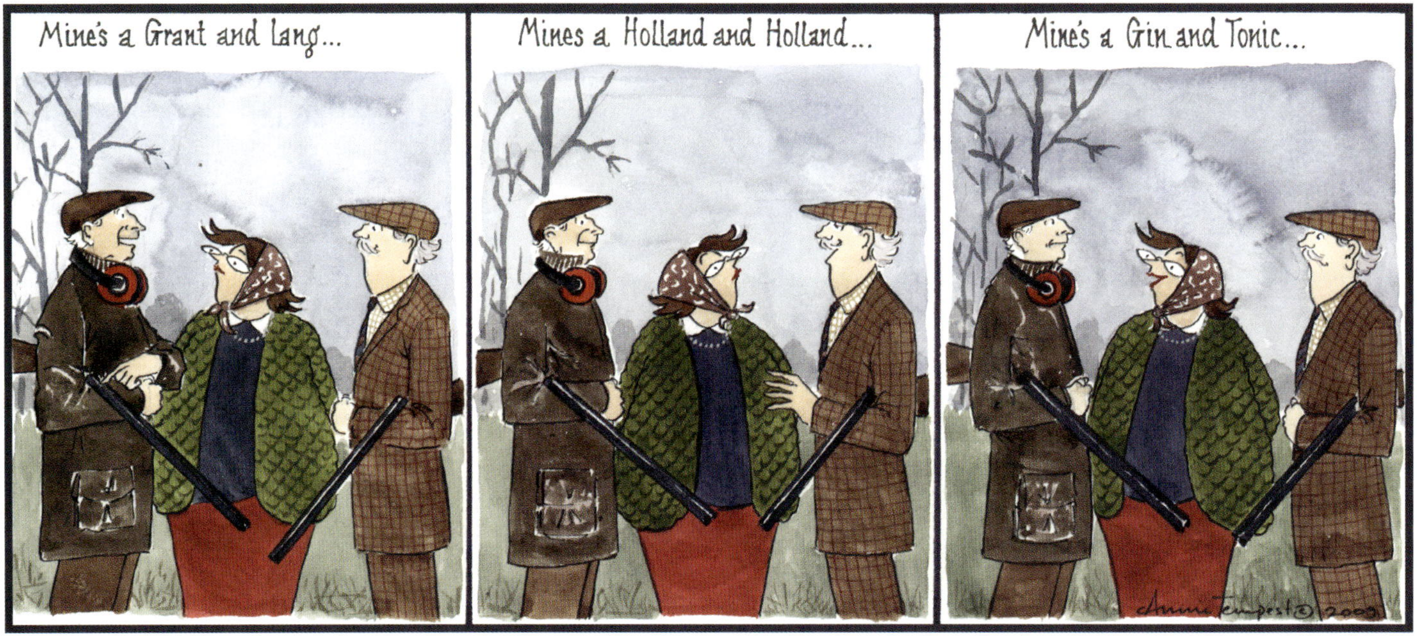
Mine's a Grant and lang...
Mines a Holland and Holland...
Mine's a Gin and Tonic...
Annie Tempest © 2009

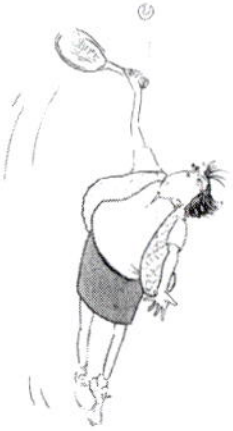

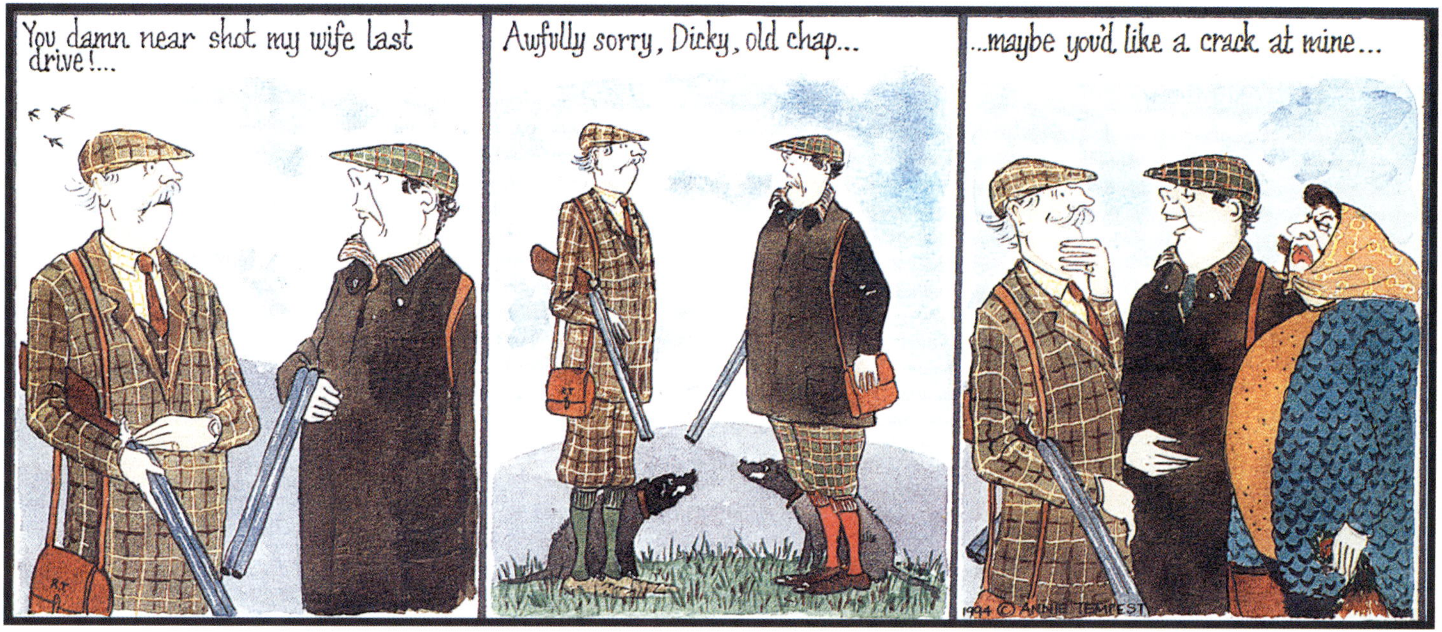
You damn near shot my wife last drive!...
Awfully sorry, Dicky, old chap...
...maybe you'd like a crack at mine...
1994 © ANNIE TEMPEST

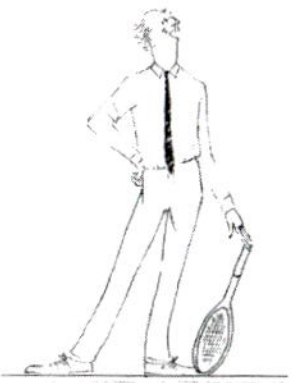

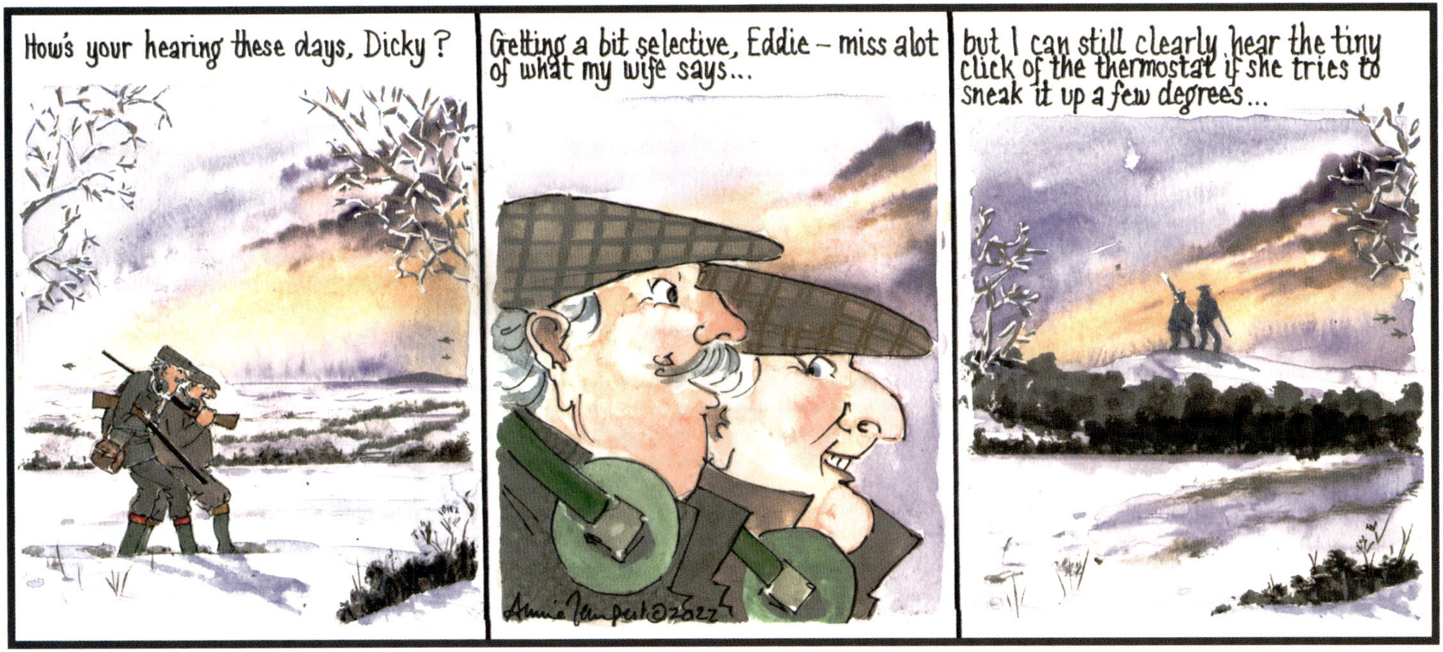
How's your hearing these days, Dicky?
Getting a bit selective, Eddie – miss alot of what my wife says...
but I can still clearly hear the tiny click of the thermostat if she tries to sneak it up a few degrees...
Annie Tempest©2022

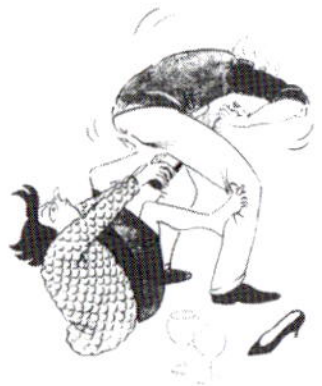

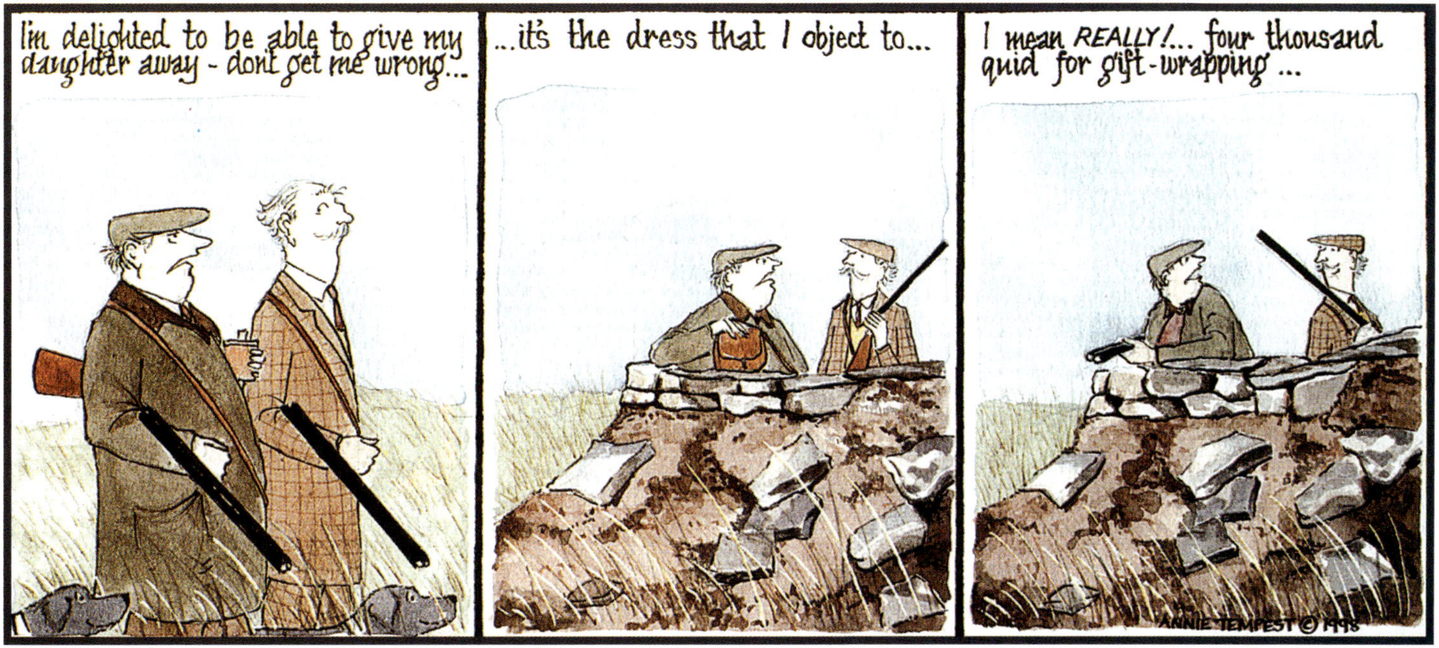
I'm delighted to be able to give my daughter away - don't get me wrong...
...it's the dress that I object to...
I mean REALLY!... four thousand quid for gift-wrapping...
ANNIE TEMPEST © 1998

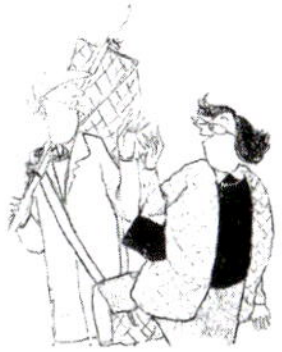

The only place one can enjoy a quiet smoke these days is on top of a moor armed with a shotgun...

An afternoon drive...

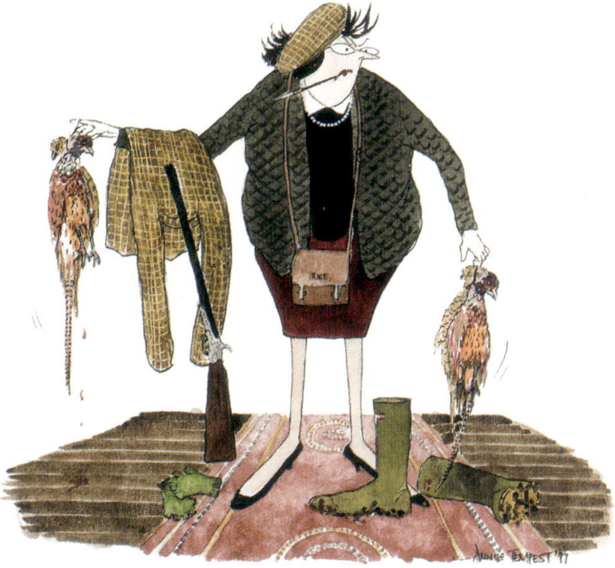
ANNIE TEMPEST '97

The gun who mistook his wife for a servant

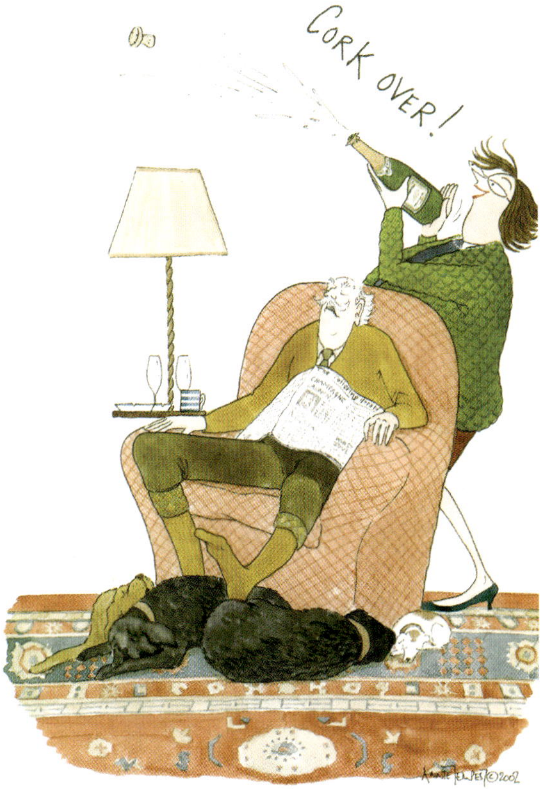
CORK OVER!
ANNIE TEMPEST ©2002

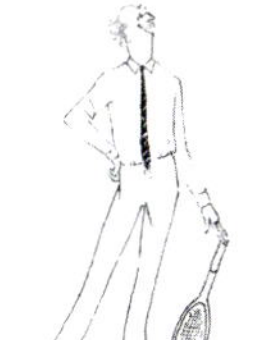

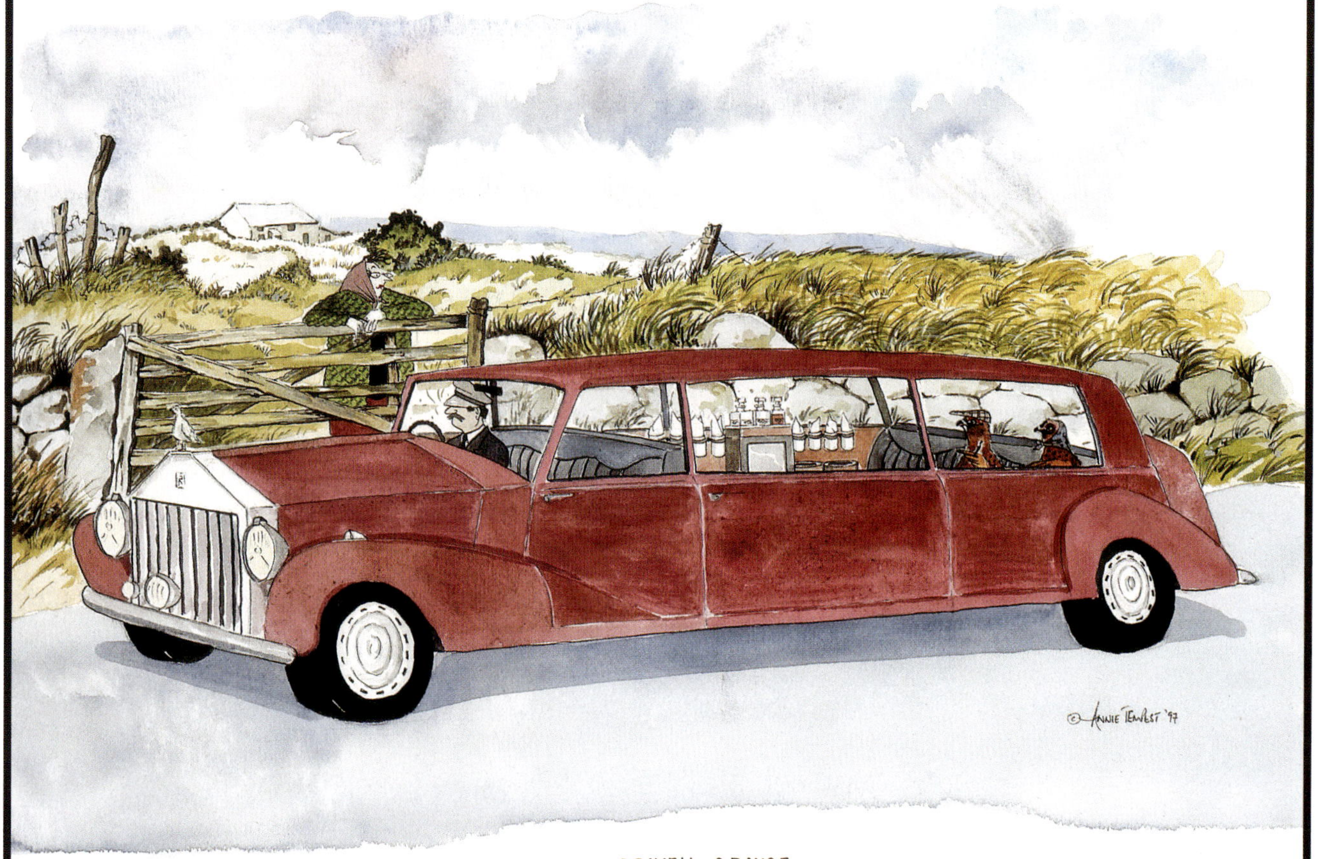
© Annie Tempest '97

DRIVEN GROUSE

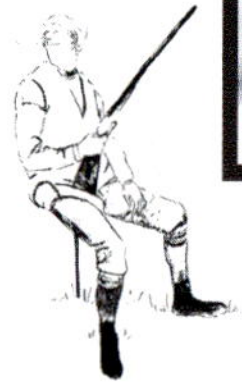

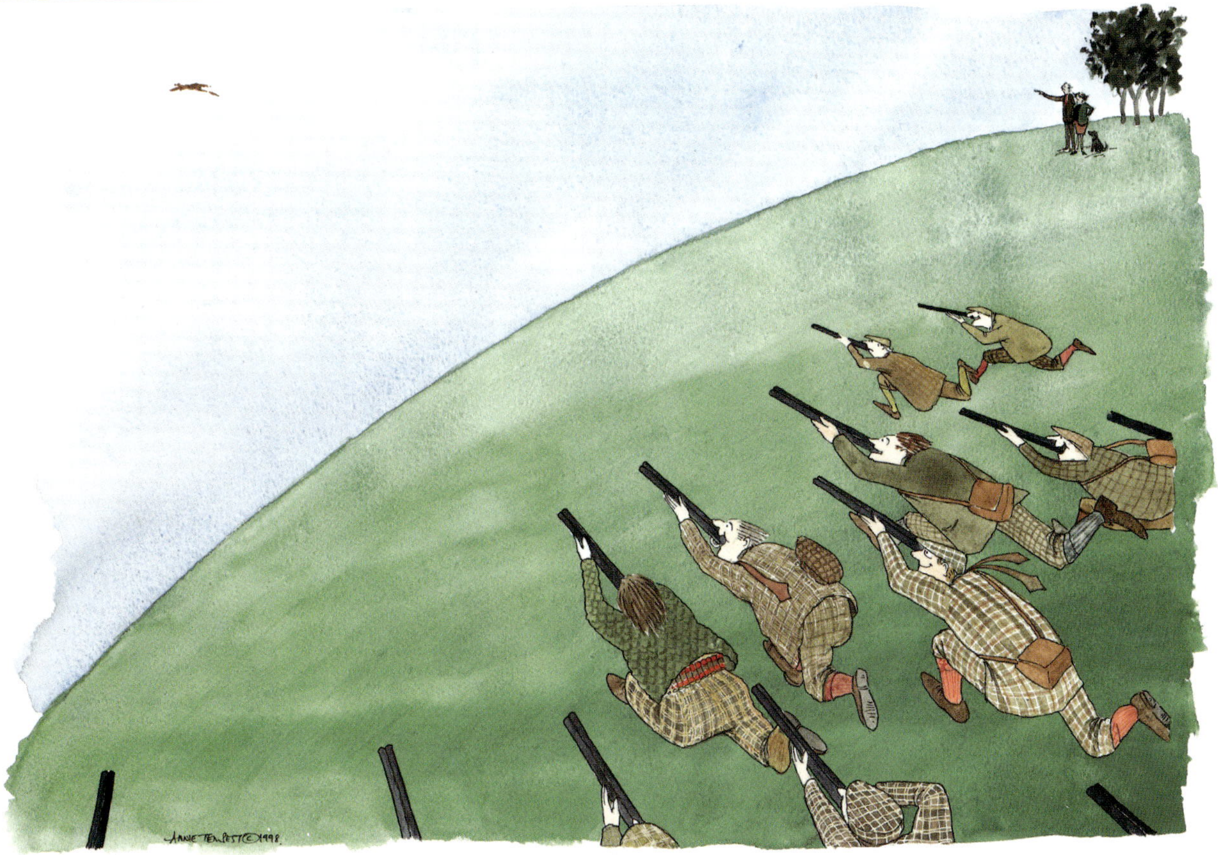
ANNIE TEMPEST © 1998.

"...THE LAST BIRD OF THE SEASON, DAFFY..."

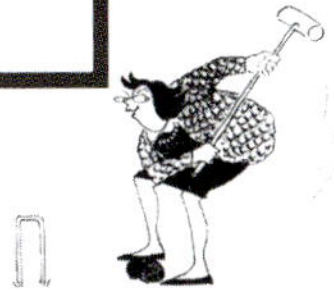

ENJOYING ONE'S HUSBAND'S HOBBIES

THE SHOOTING SEASON – "CORK OVER!"

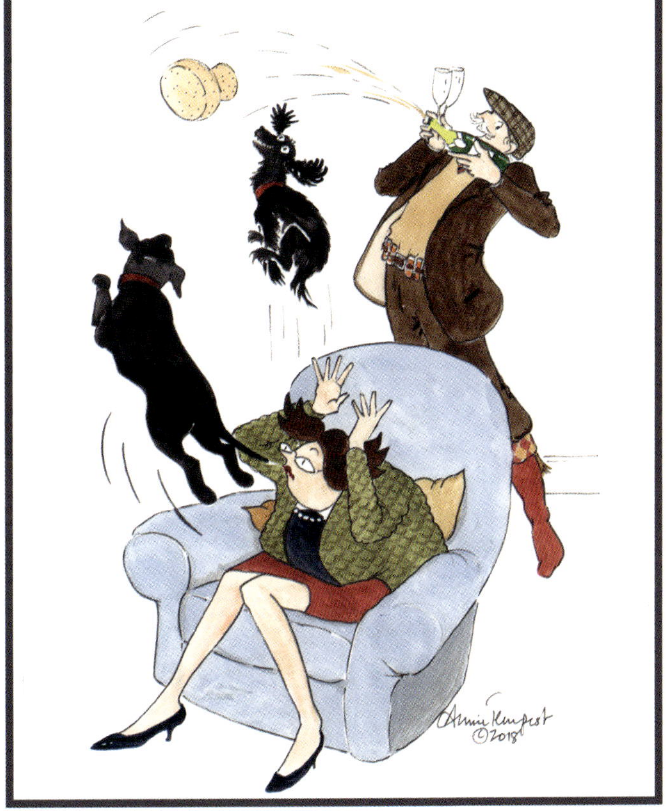
Annie Tempest
©2018

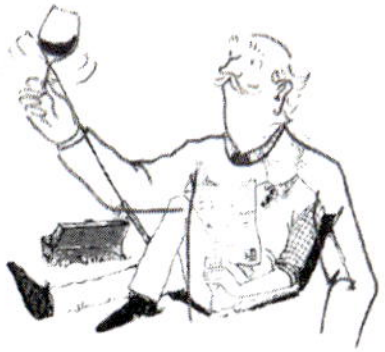

Zi-PurDey-Doo-Dah!

"I suppose I've under topped the odd keeper and had a few low birds…"

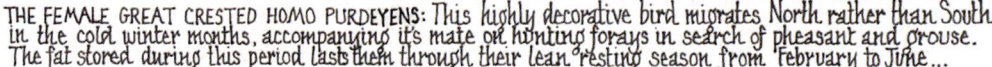

THE FEMALE GREAT CRESTED HOMO PURDEYENS: This highly decorative bird migrates North rather than South in the cold winter months, accompanying it's mate on hunting forays in search of pheasant and grouse. The fat stored during this period lasts them through their lean resting season from February to June...

'There are lane closures in both directions at South Pimms with traffic tailing back to Havock in the Wreake and Waddles End. Engineering work is disrupting First TransPimmshire trains on all routes with replacement bus services between Mugglesford and Rottingbeam...'

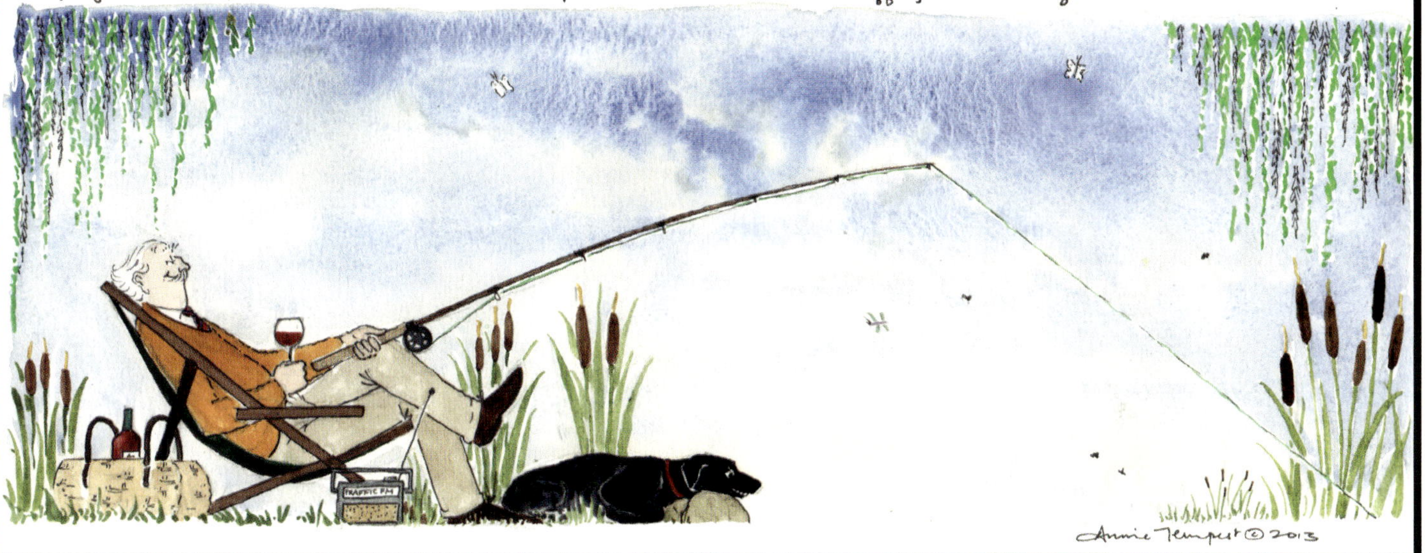
TRAFFIC FM
Annie Tempest © 2013

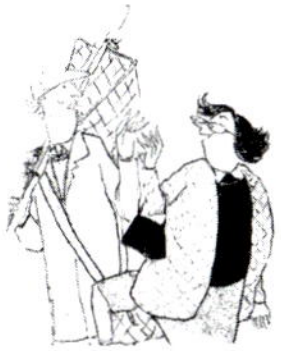

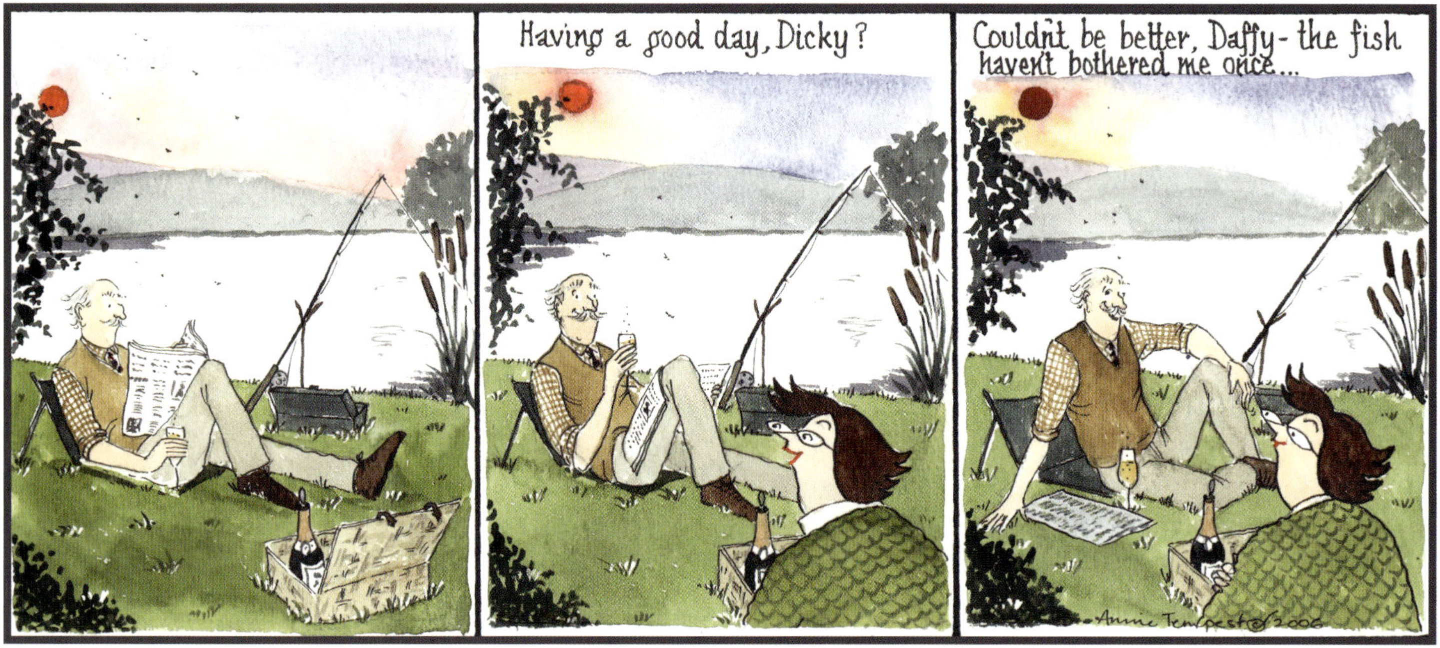
Having a good day, Dicky?
Couldn't be better, Daffy- the fish haven't bothered me once...
Annie Tempest ©2006

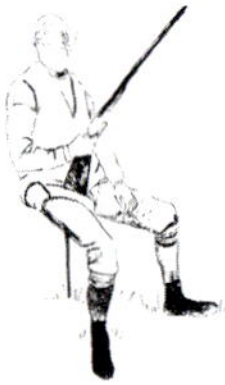

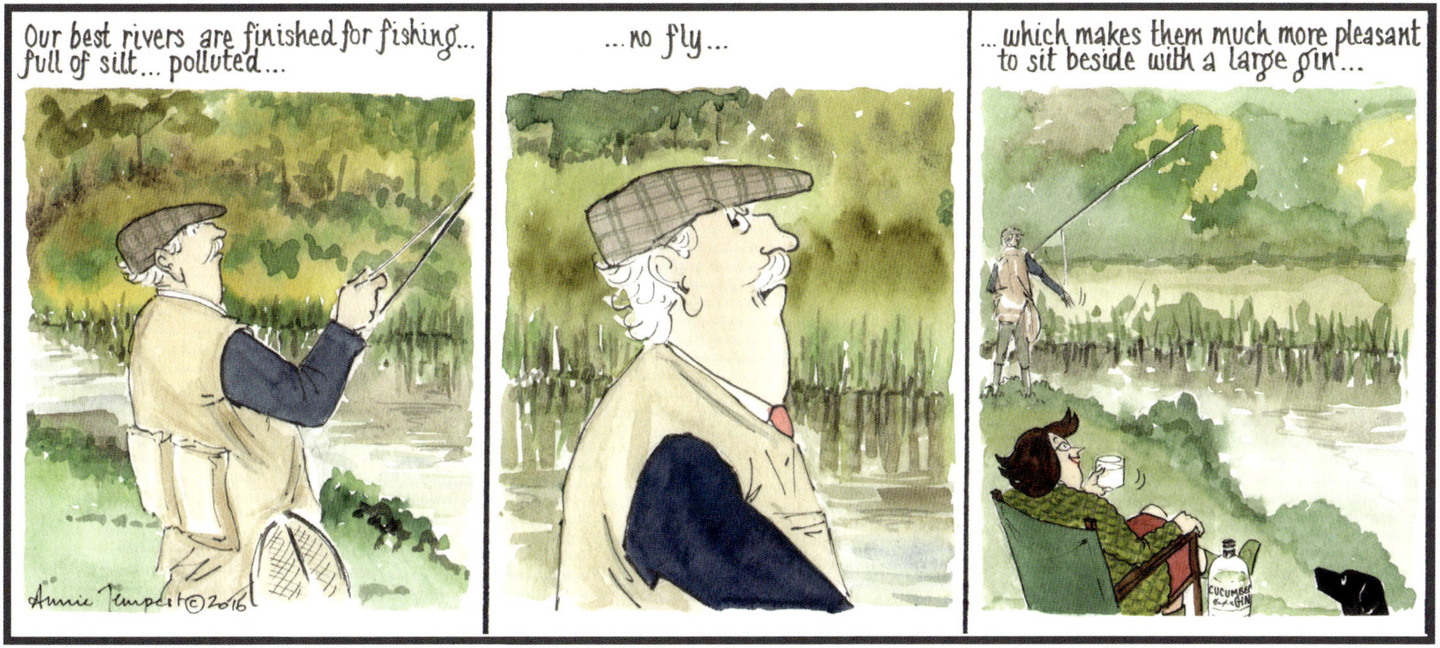
Our best rivers are finished for fishing...
full of silt... polluted...
...no fly...
...which makes them much more pleasant
to sit beside with a large gin...
Annie Tempest © 2016
CUCUMBER
GIN

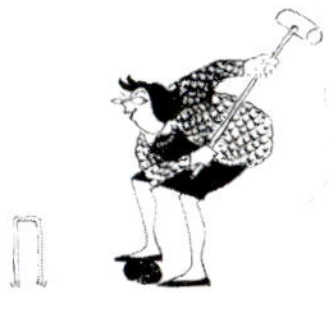

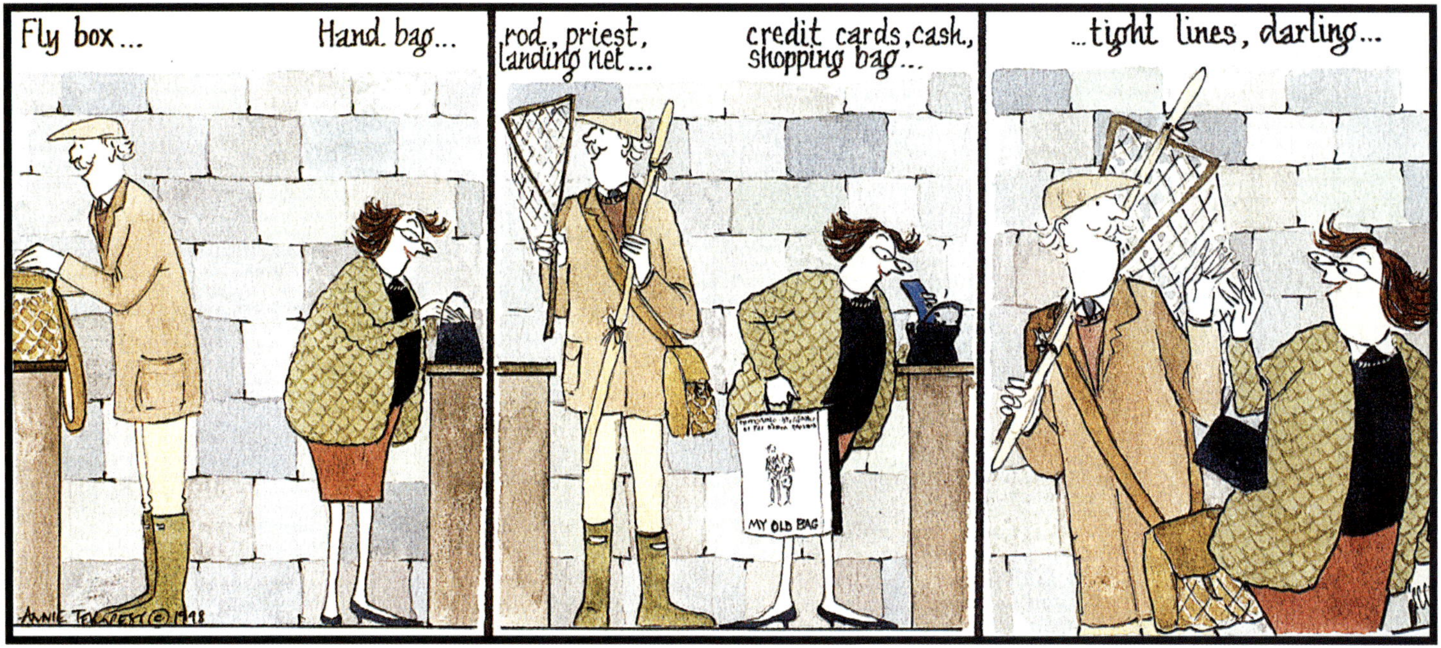
Fly box...
Hand bag...
rod, priest, landing net...
credit cards, cash, shopping bag...
MY OLD BAG
...tight lines, darling...
ANNIE TEMPEST © 1998

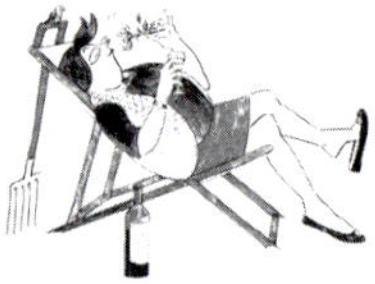

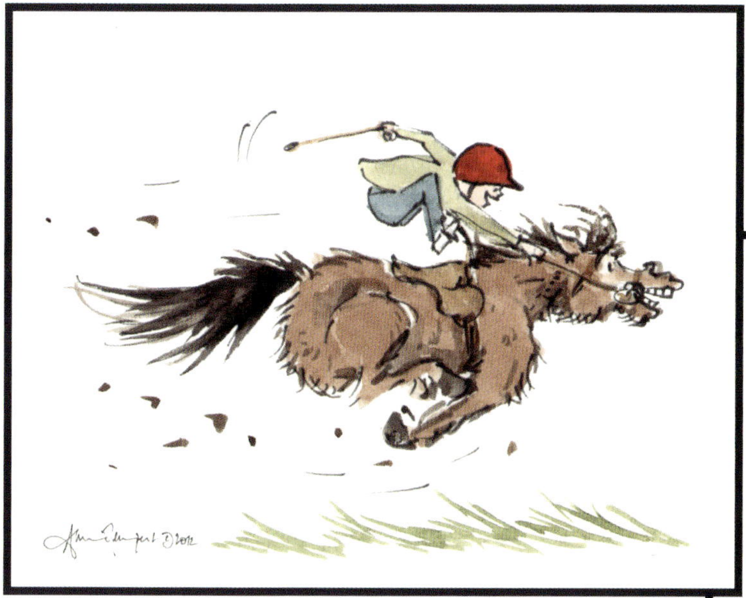

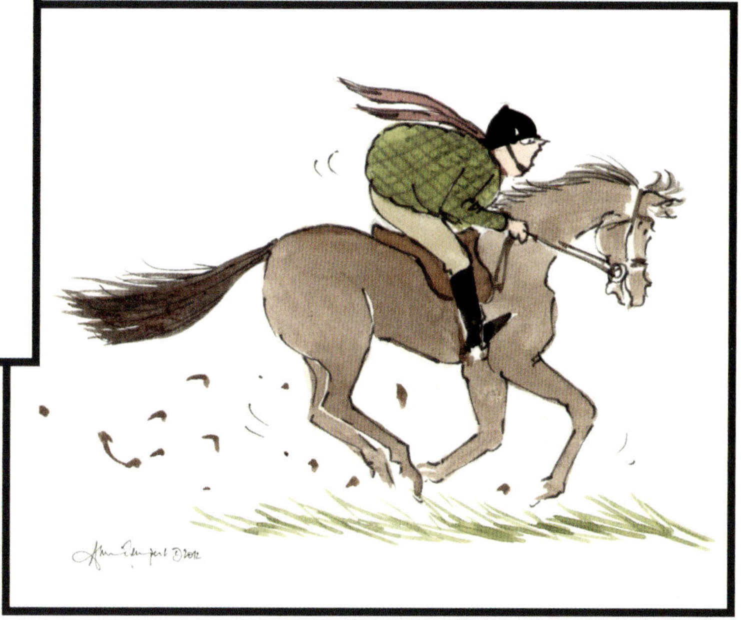

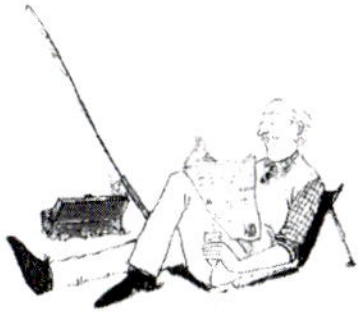

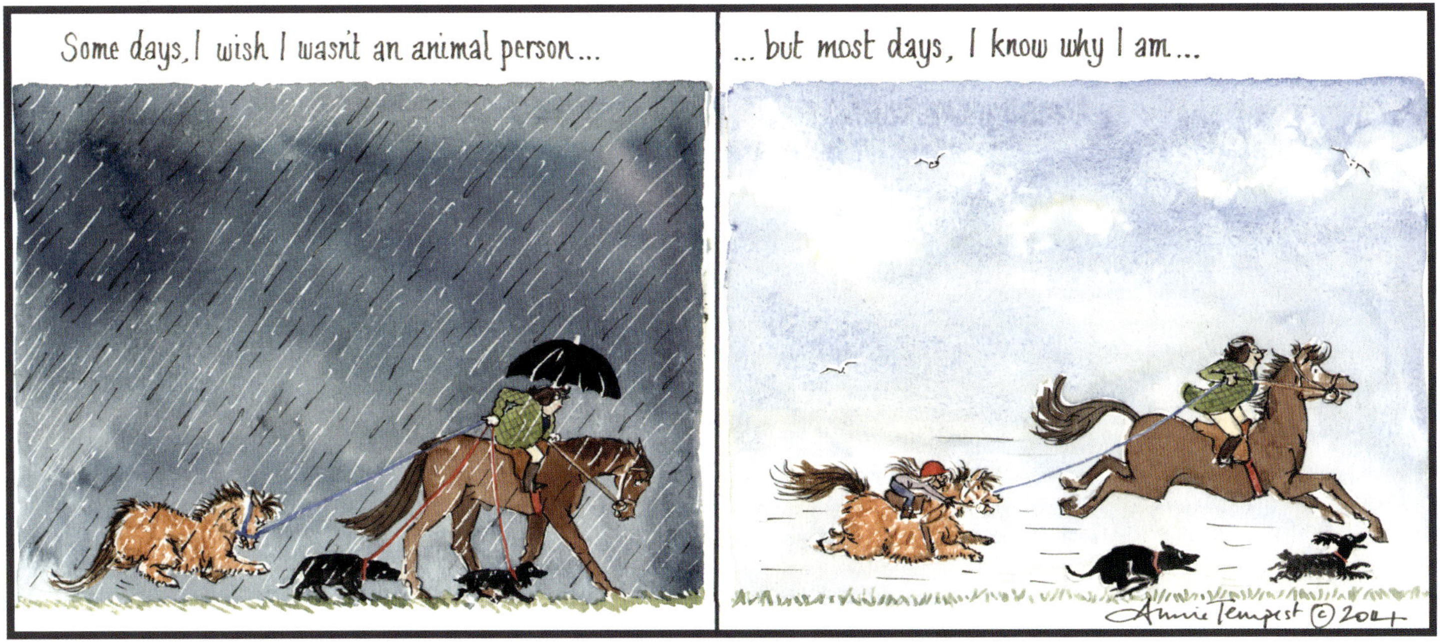
Some days, I wish I wasn't an animal person...
... but most days, I know why I am...
Annie Tempest © 2014

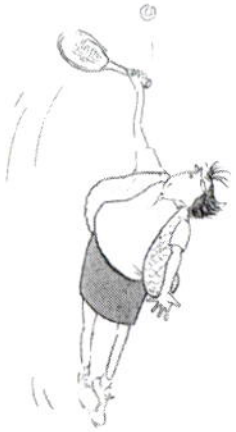

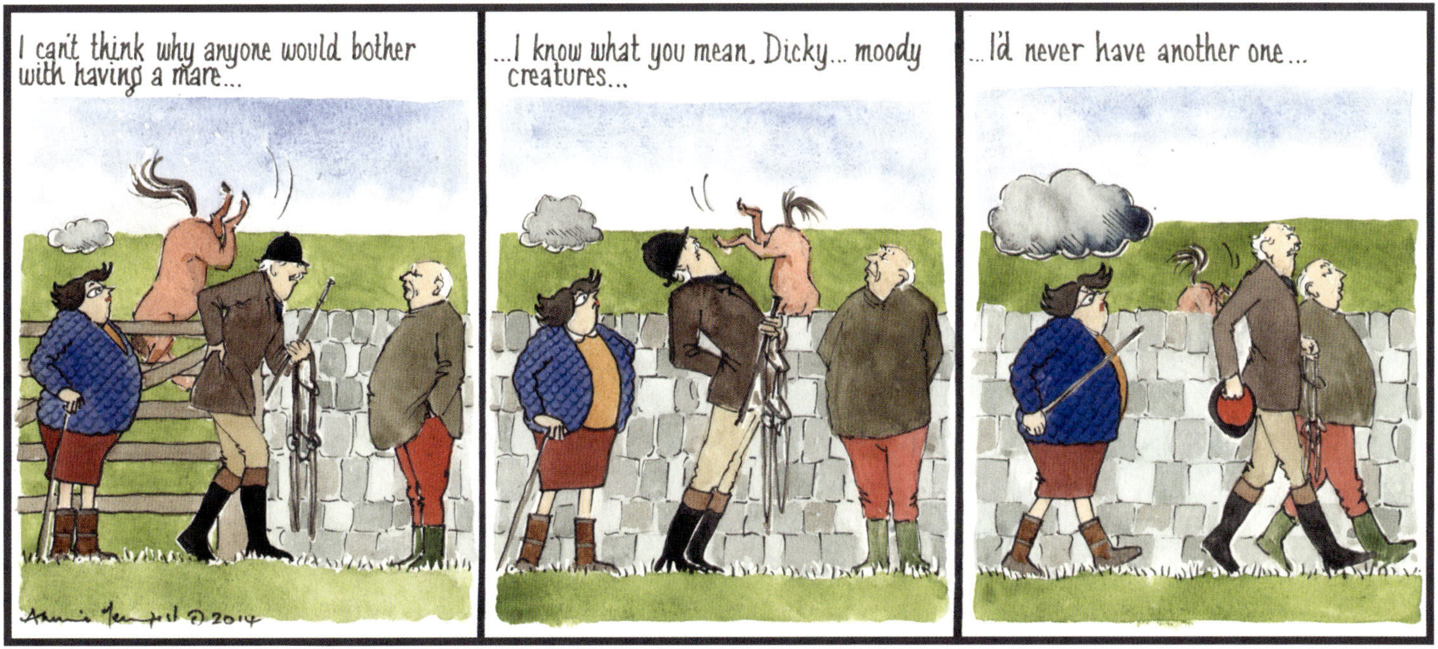
I can't think why anyone would bother with having a mare...
...I know what you mean, Dicky... moody creatures...
...I'd never have another one...

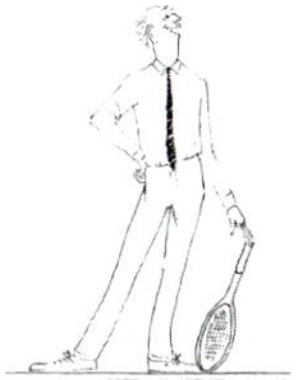

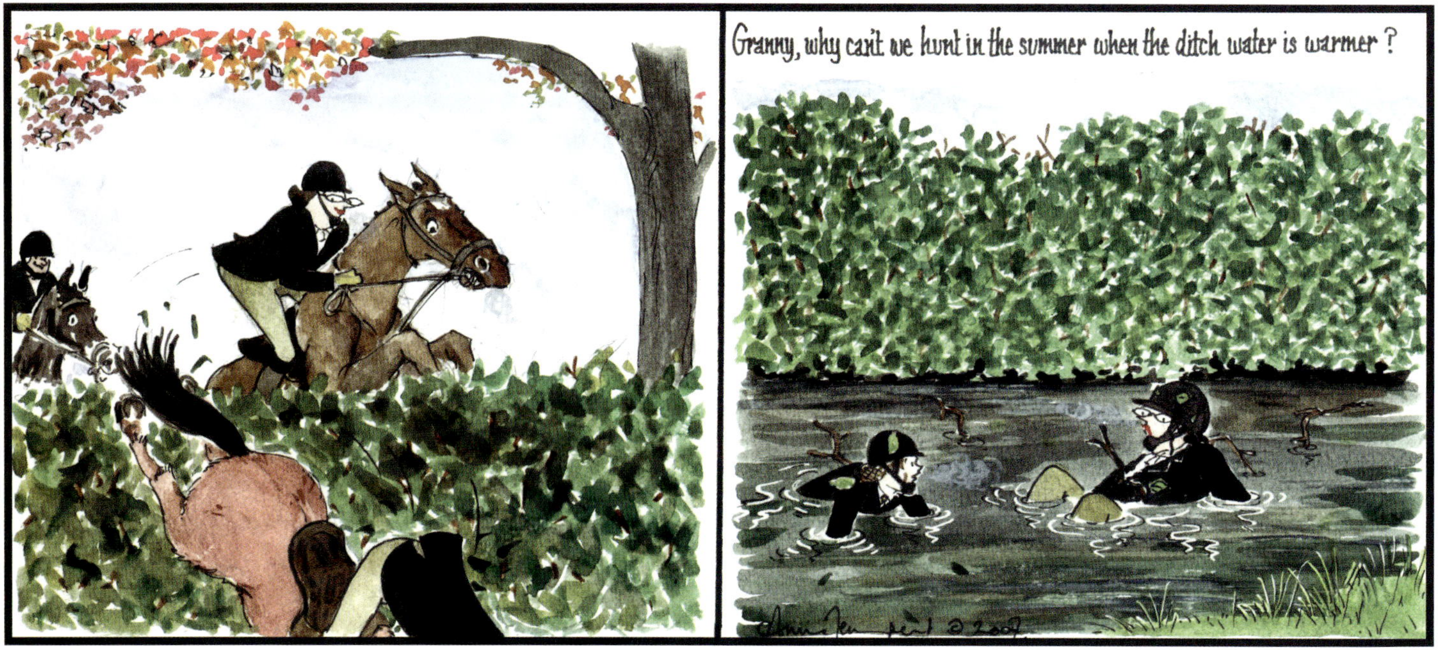
Granny, why can't we hunt in the summer when the ditch water is warmer ?

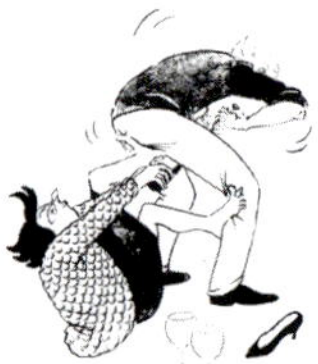

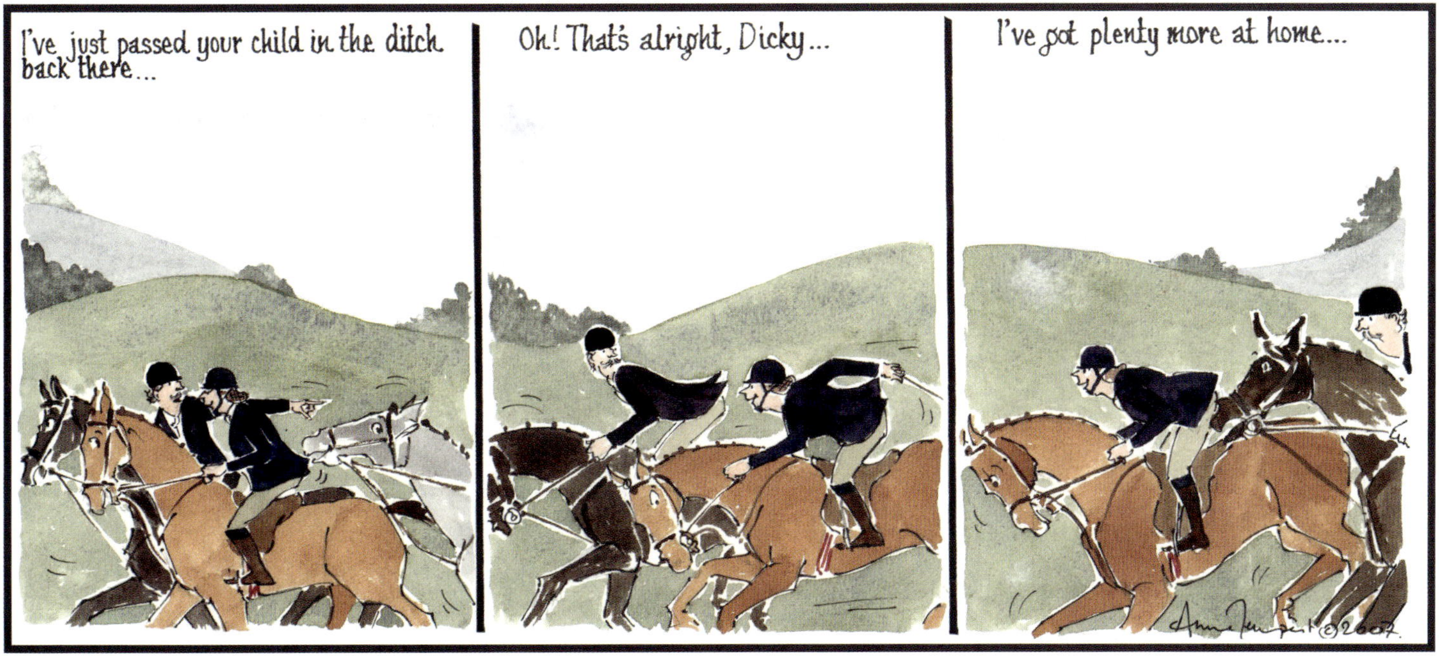
I've just passed your child in the ditch back there...
Oh! That's alright, Dicky...
I've got plenty more at home...

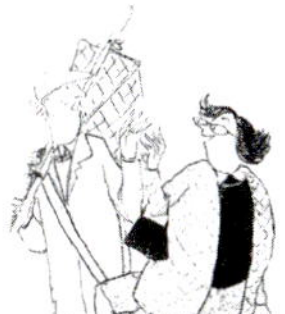

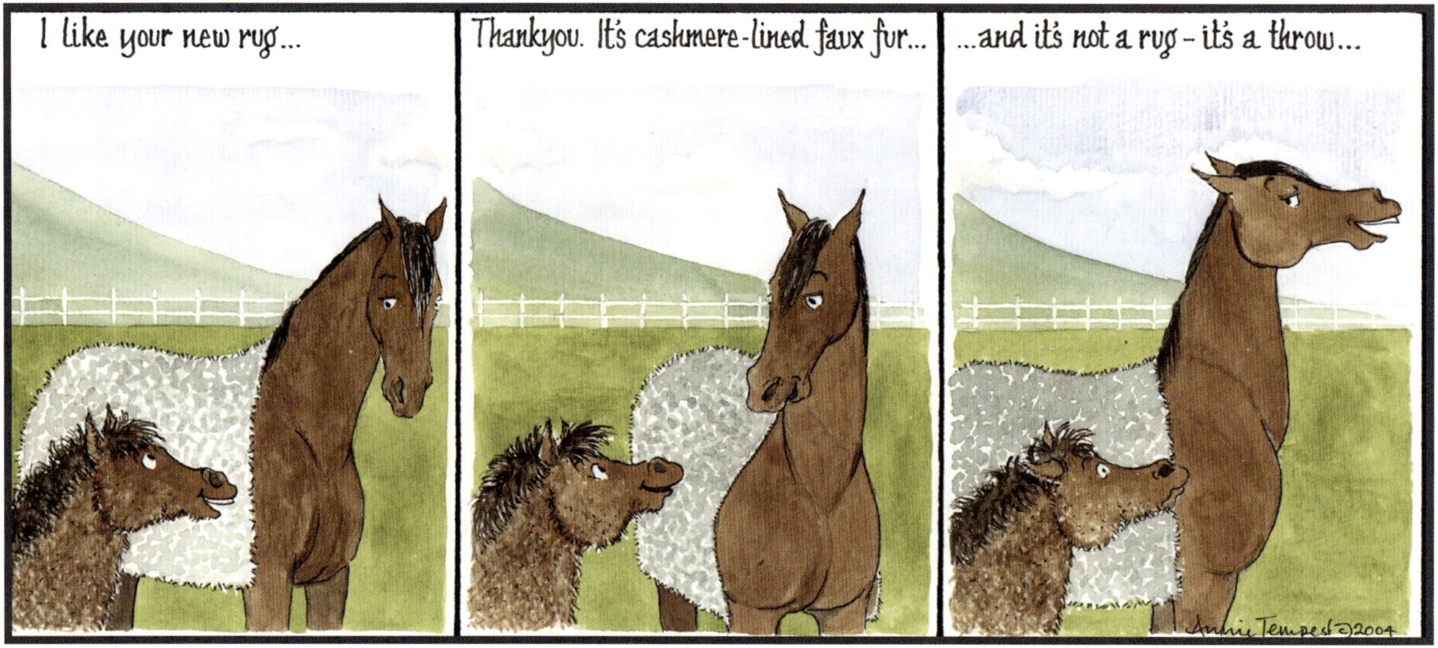
I like your new rug...
Thankyou. It's cashmere-lined faux fur...
...and it's not a rug - it's a throw...
Annie Tempest ©2004

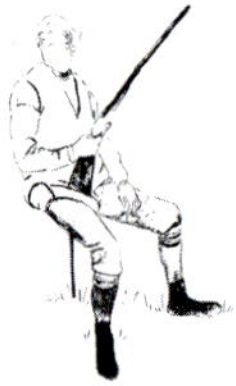

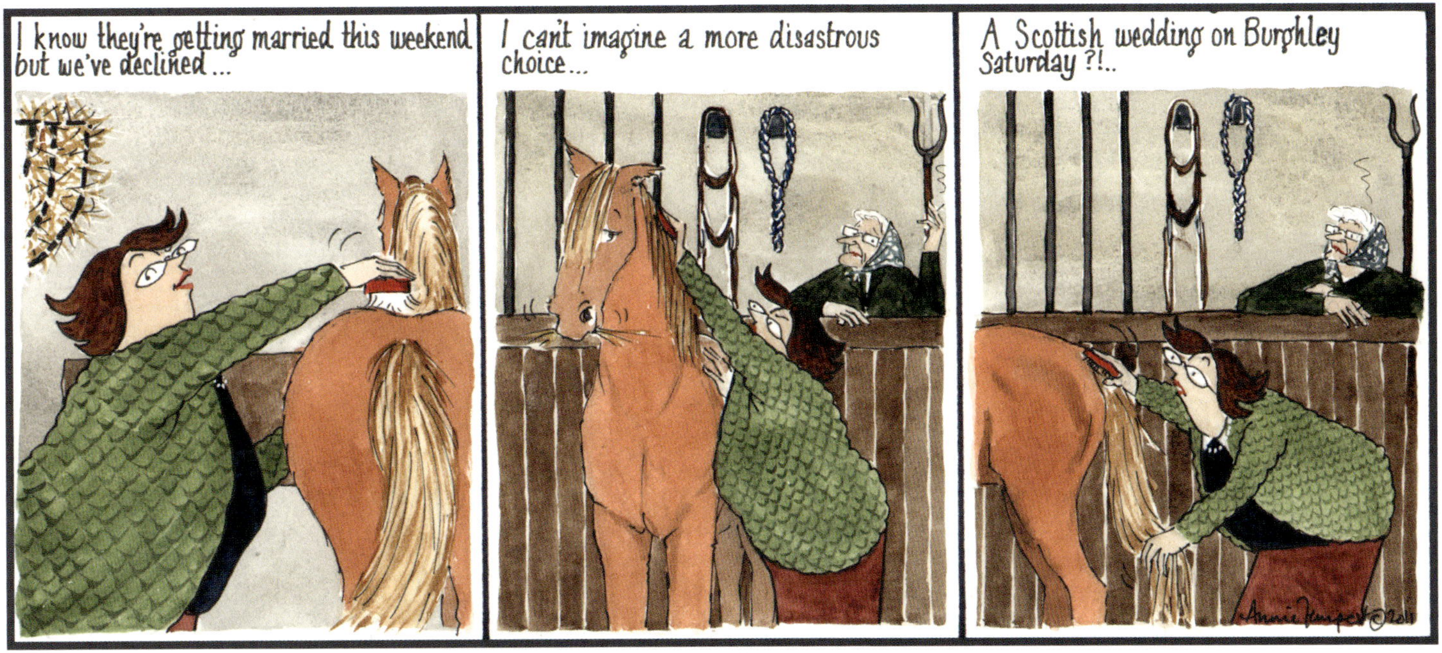
I know they're getting married this weekend but we've declined ...
I can't imagine a more disastrous choice...
A Scottish wedding on Burghley Saturday ?!..

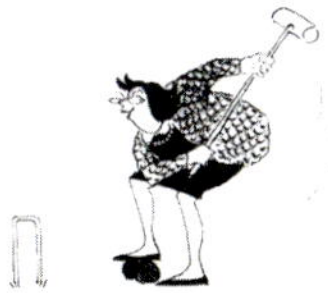

THE 'TWEED-CLAD FOSSILS' OF CHELTENHAM RACES ARE A HARDY BREED.

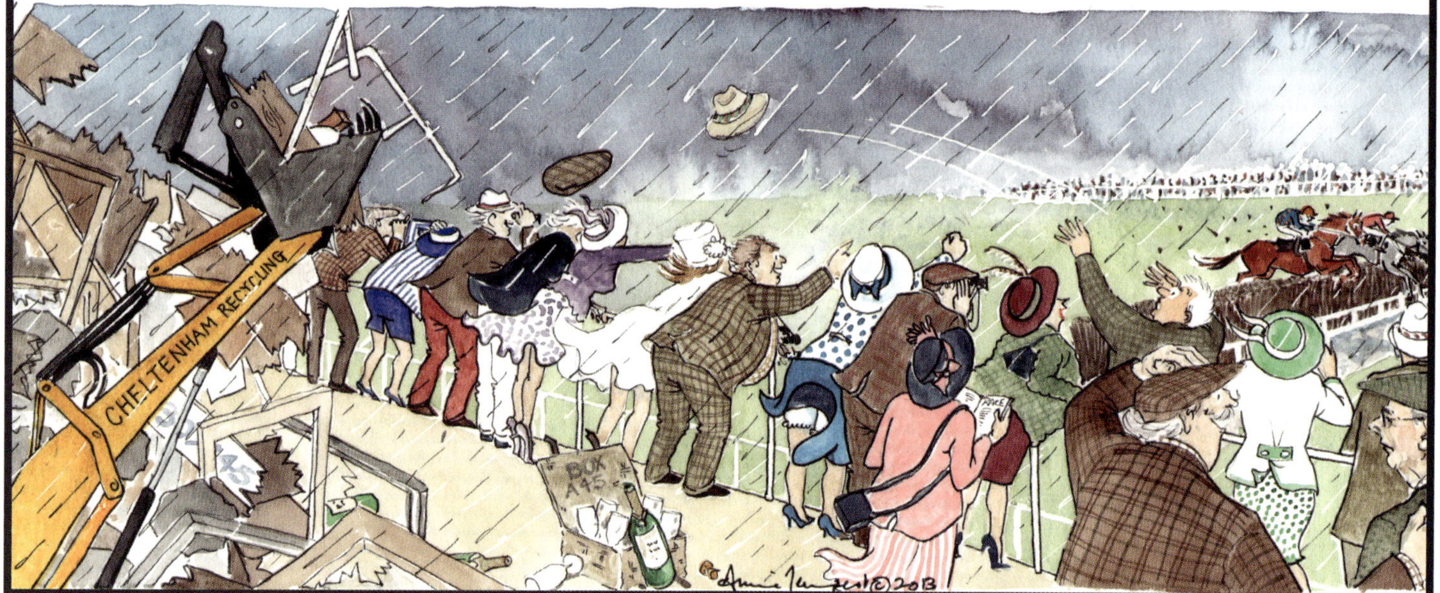
CHELTENHAM RECYCLING
BOX A45
RACE
© 2013

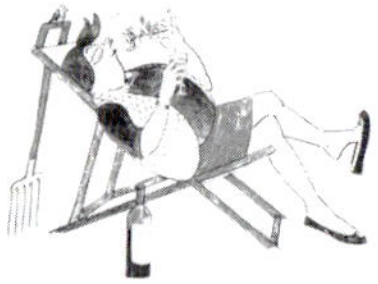

Damn pony's spotted that low branch ... hope we've got enough petrol for a trip into A & E again ...

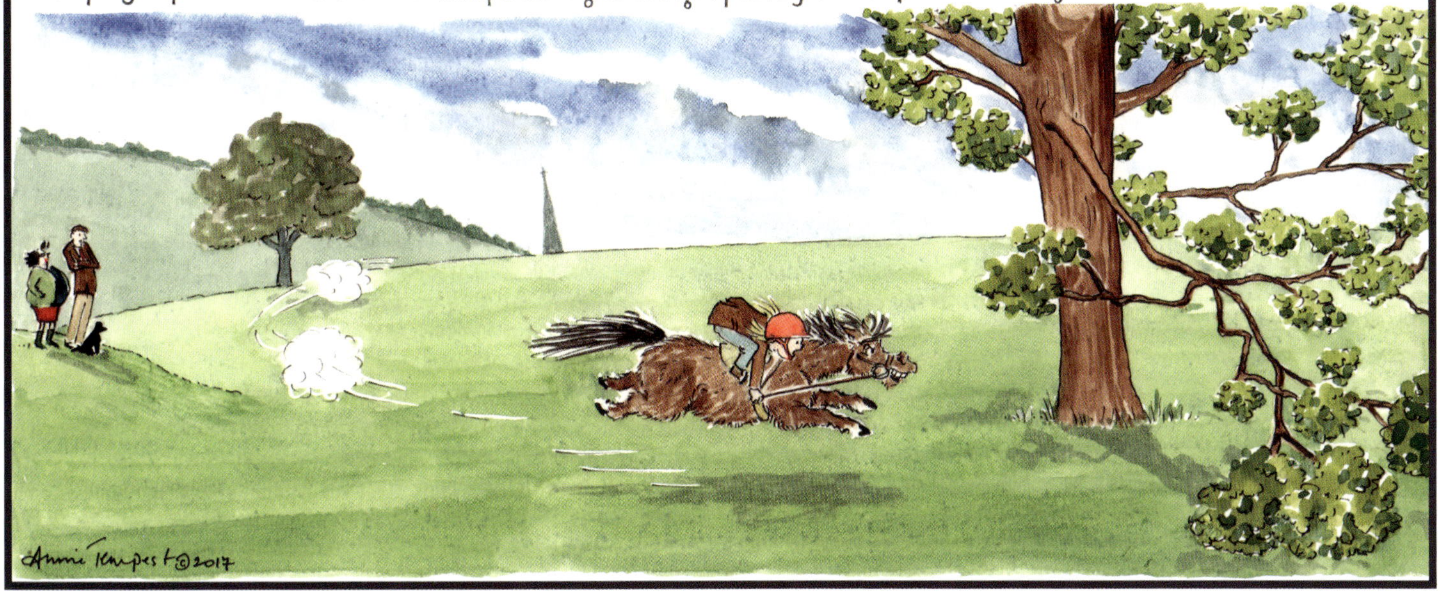
Annie Tempest ©2017

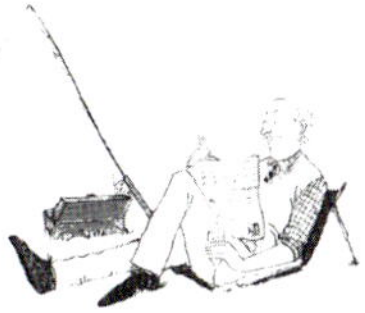

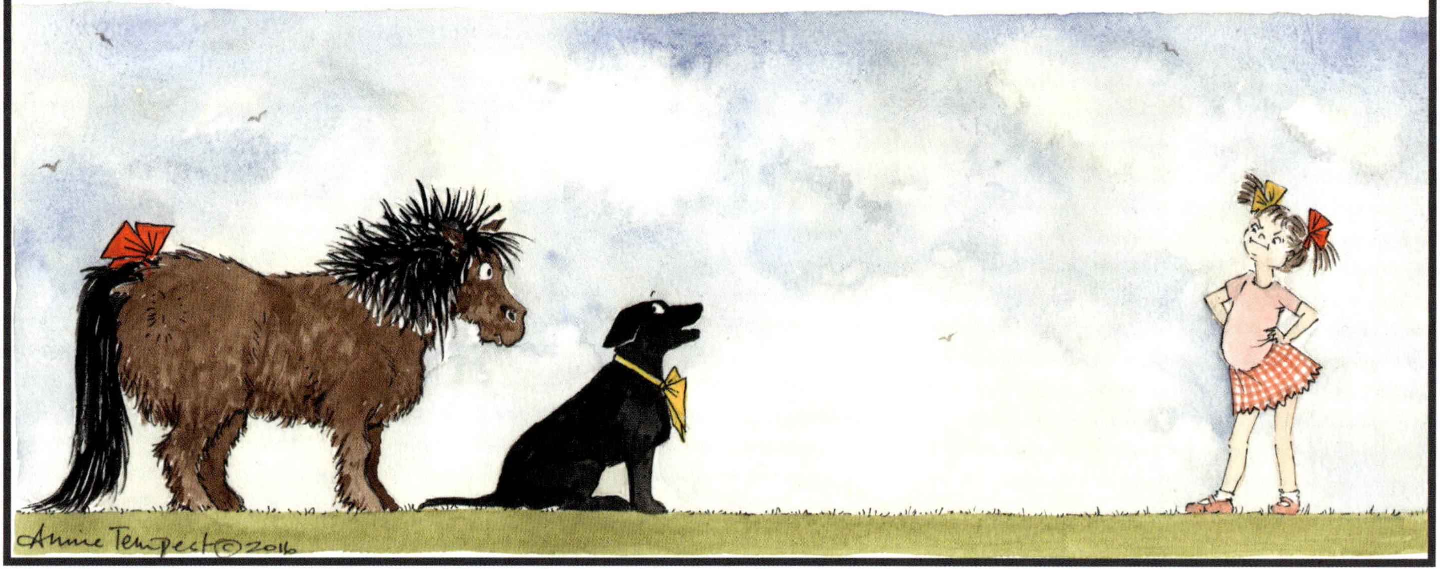
Annie Tempest © 2016

"If your red ribbon means you're a good kicker and my yellow ribbon means I'm a good biter..."

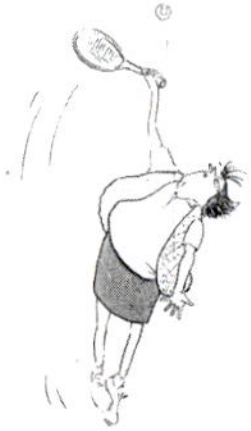

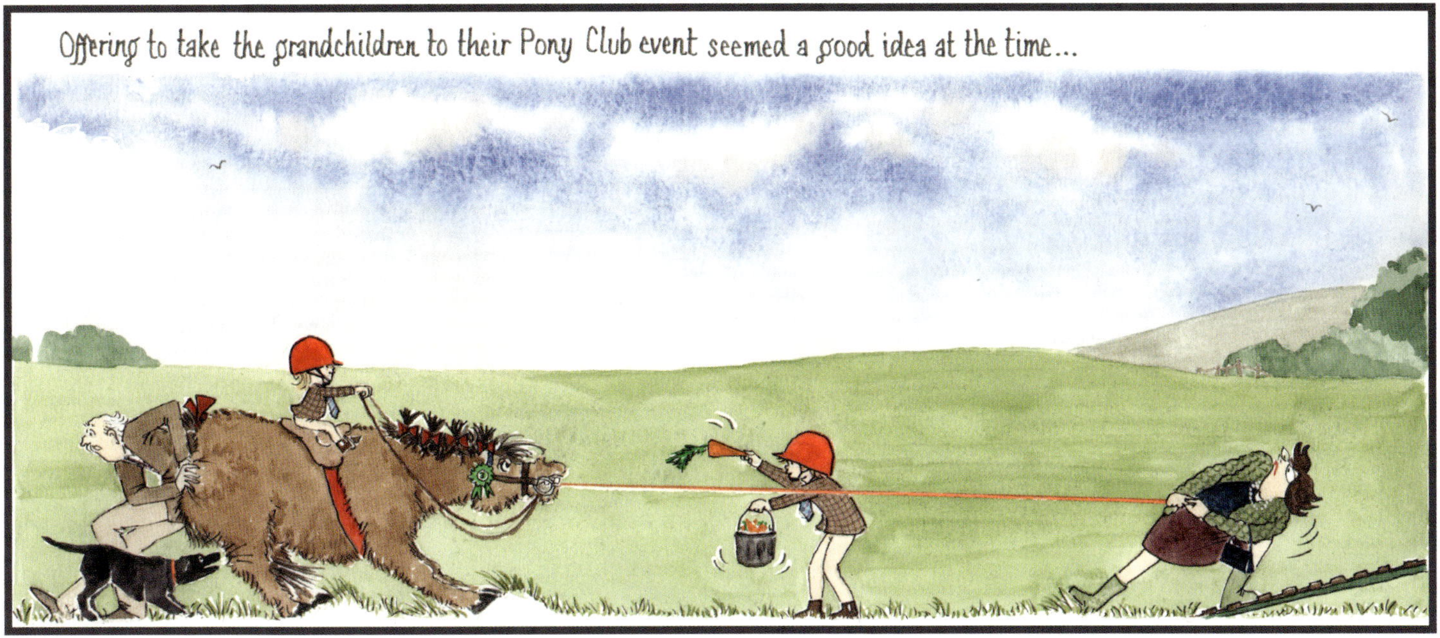

Offering to take the grandchildren to their Pony Club event seemed a good idea at the time...

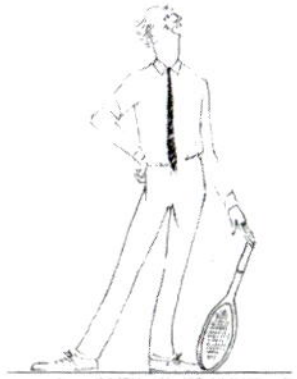

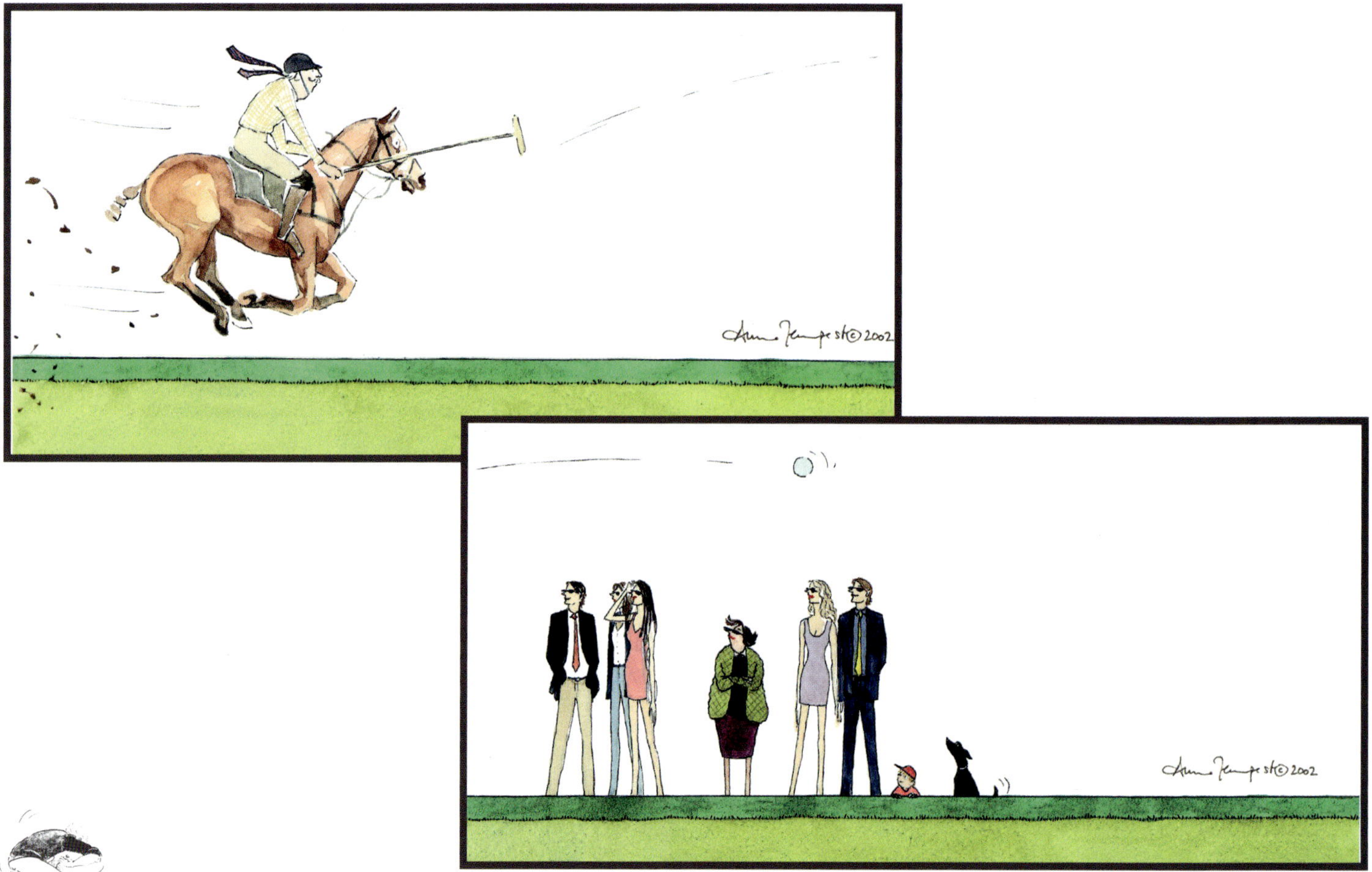

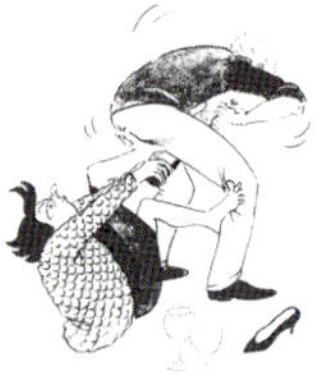

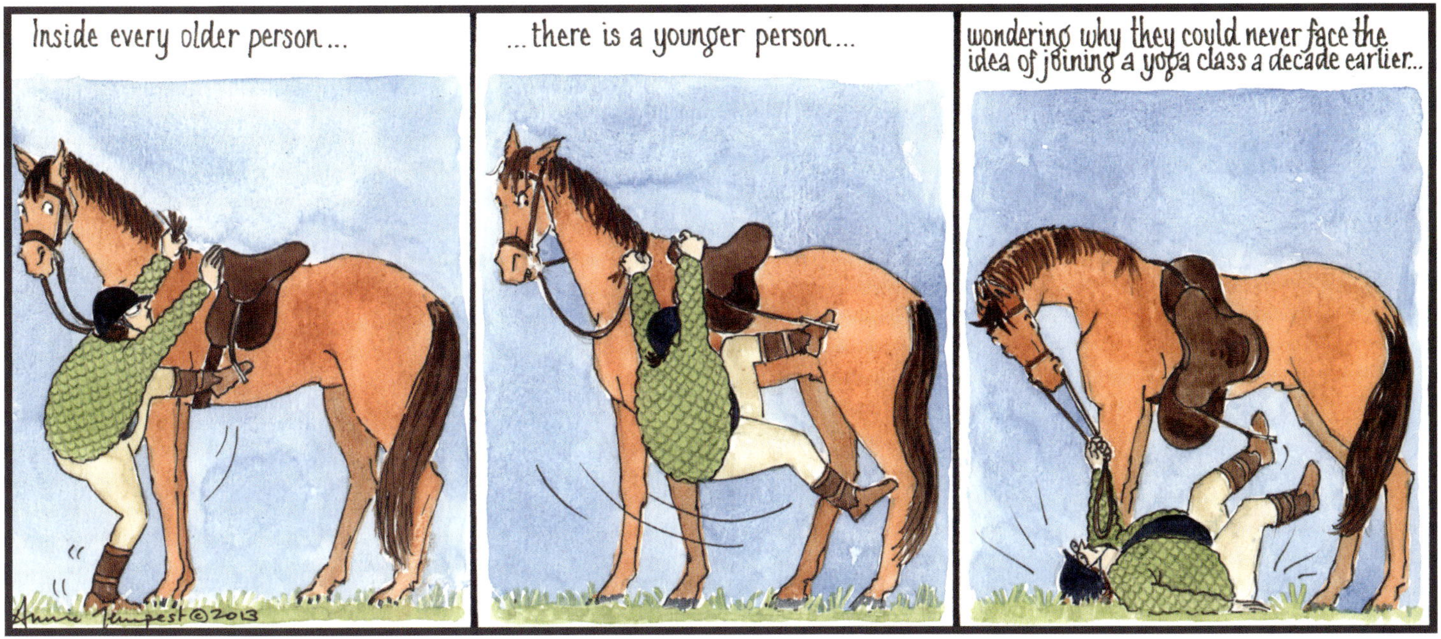
Inside every older person...
...there is a younger person...
wondering why they could never face the idea of joining a yoga class a decade earlier...
Annie Tempest ©2013

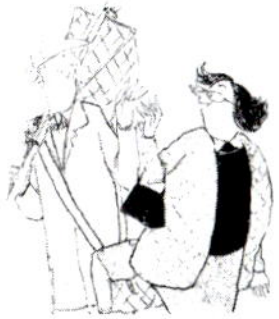

"I can't believe you're cancelling a day's hunting over a few showers..."

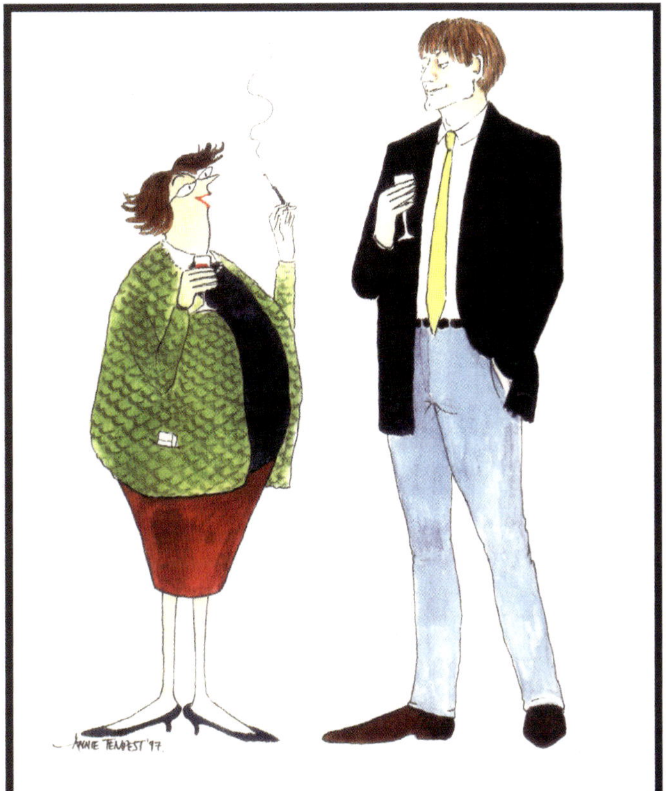
ANNIE TEMPEST '97

"Dicky used to play polo at Kirtlington but the only contact sport I've ever gone in for is parking in Chelsea..."

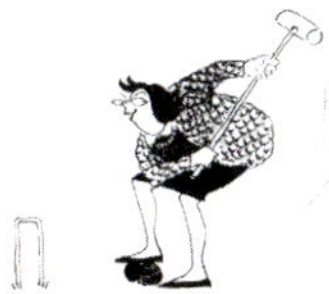

"It's much quicker if you just pick the ball up and stick it in the hole. There! Can we go for lunch now?"

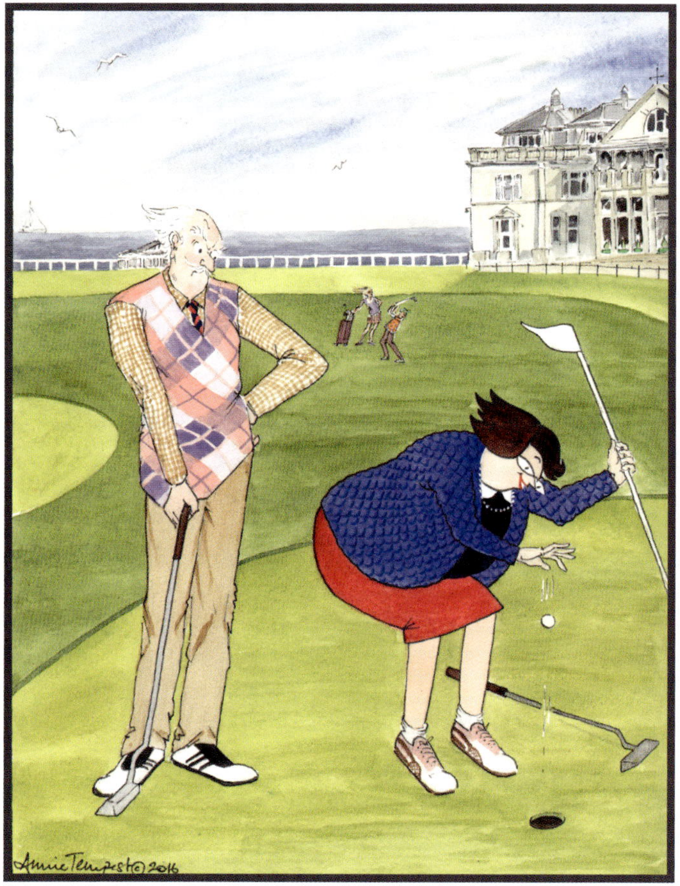
Annie Tempest © 2016

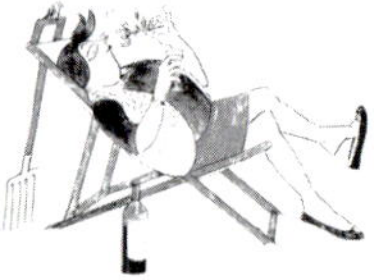

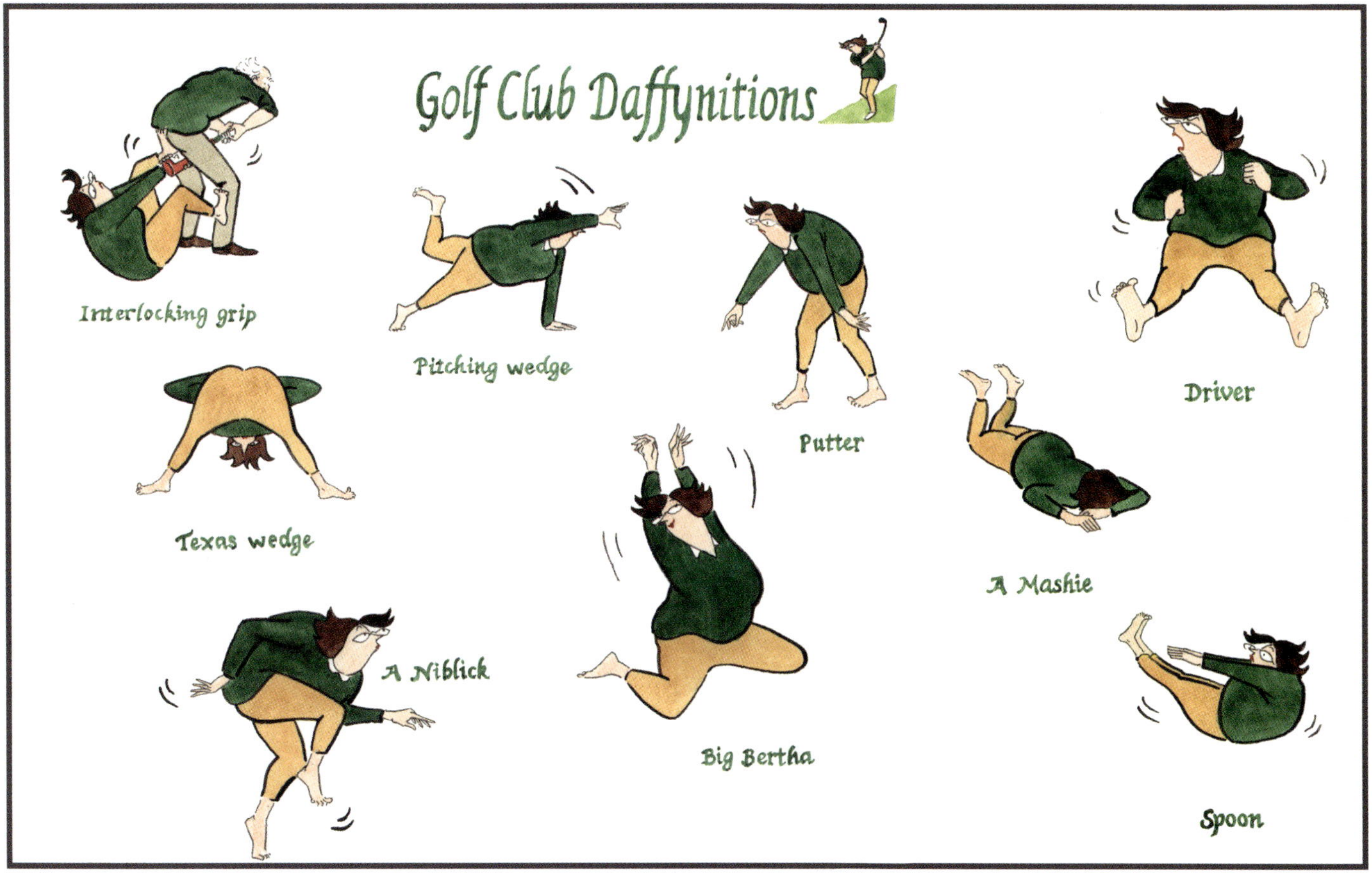
Golf Club Daffynitions
Interlocking grip
Pitching wedge
Putter
Driver
Texas wedge
A Mashie
Big Bertha
A Niblick
Spoon

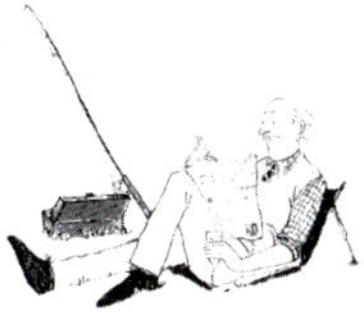

"Look children! Scribble's found a little beach out of the wind for our pic-nic ..."

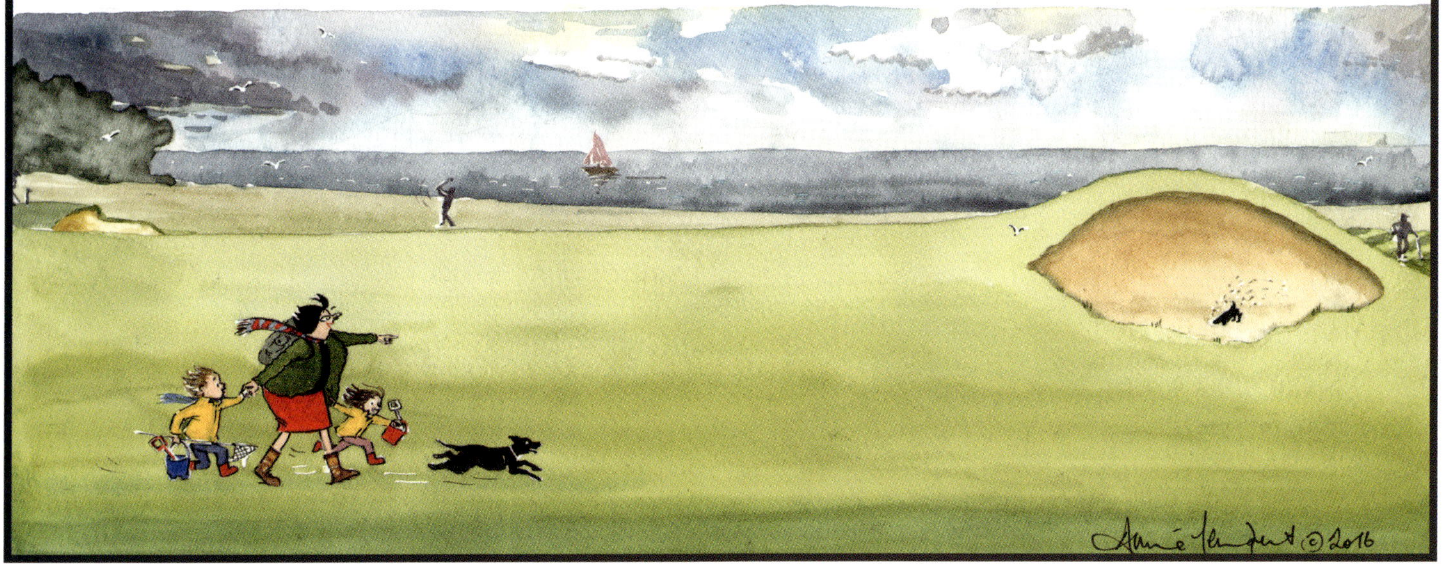
Annie Tempest © 2016

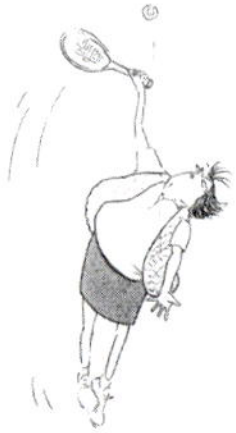

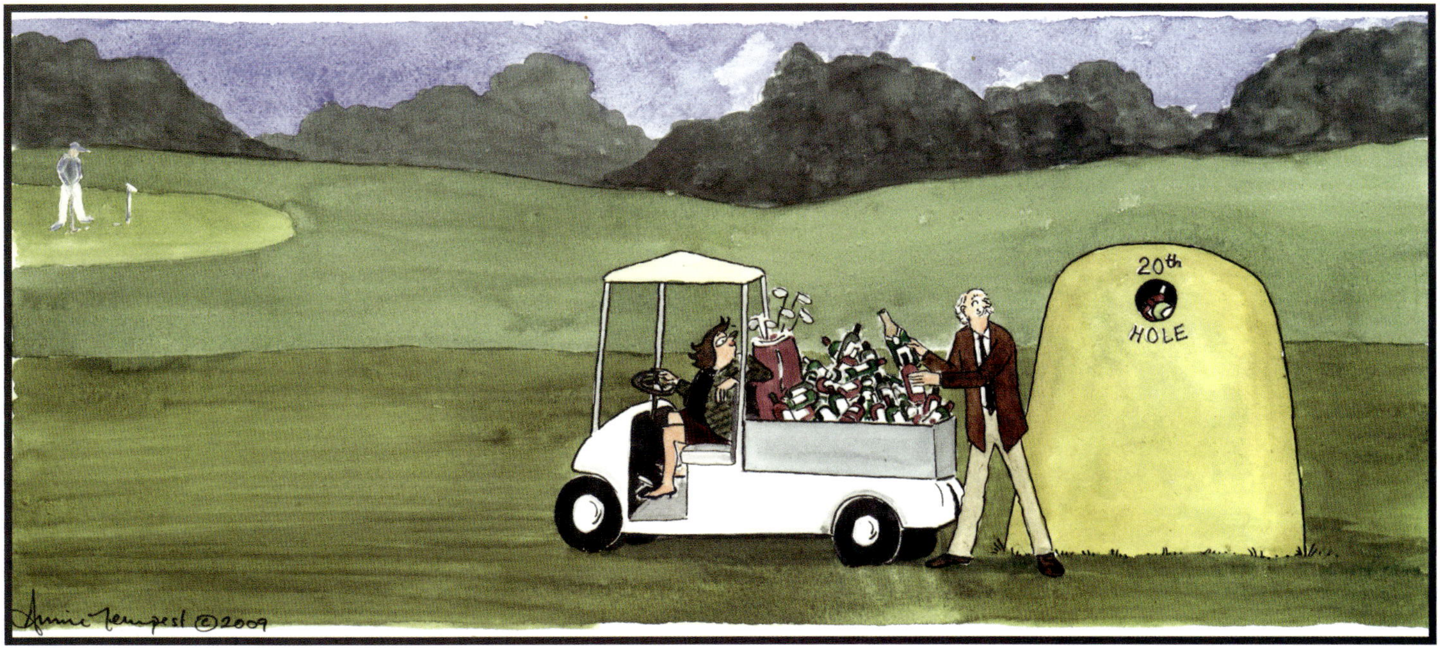
20th
HOLE
Annie Tempest ©2009

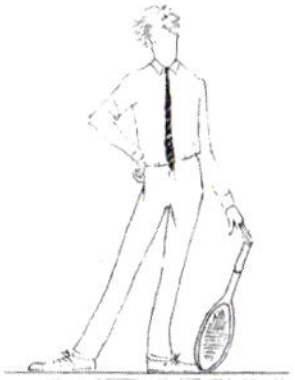

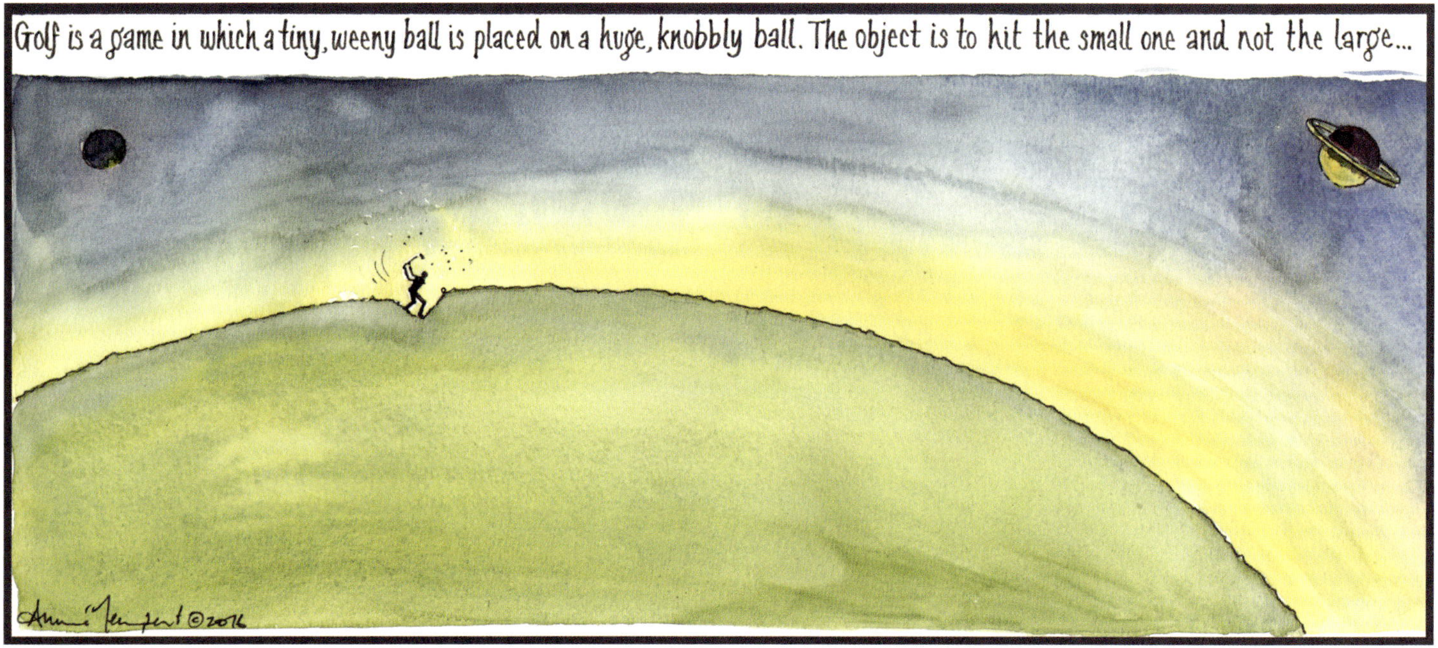
Golf is a game in which a tiny, weeny ball is placed on a huge, knobbly ball. The object is to hit the small one and not the large...

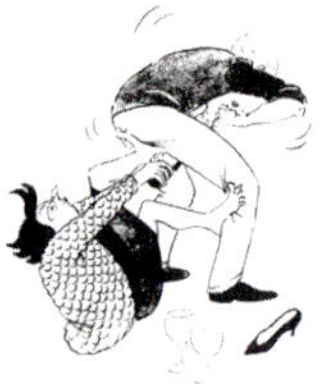

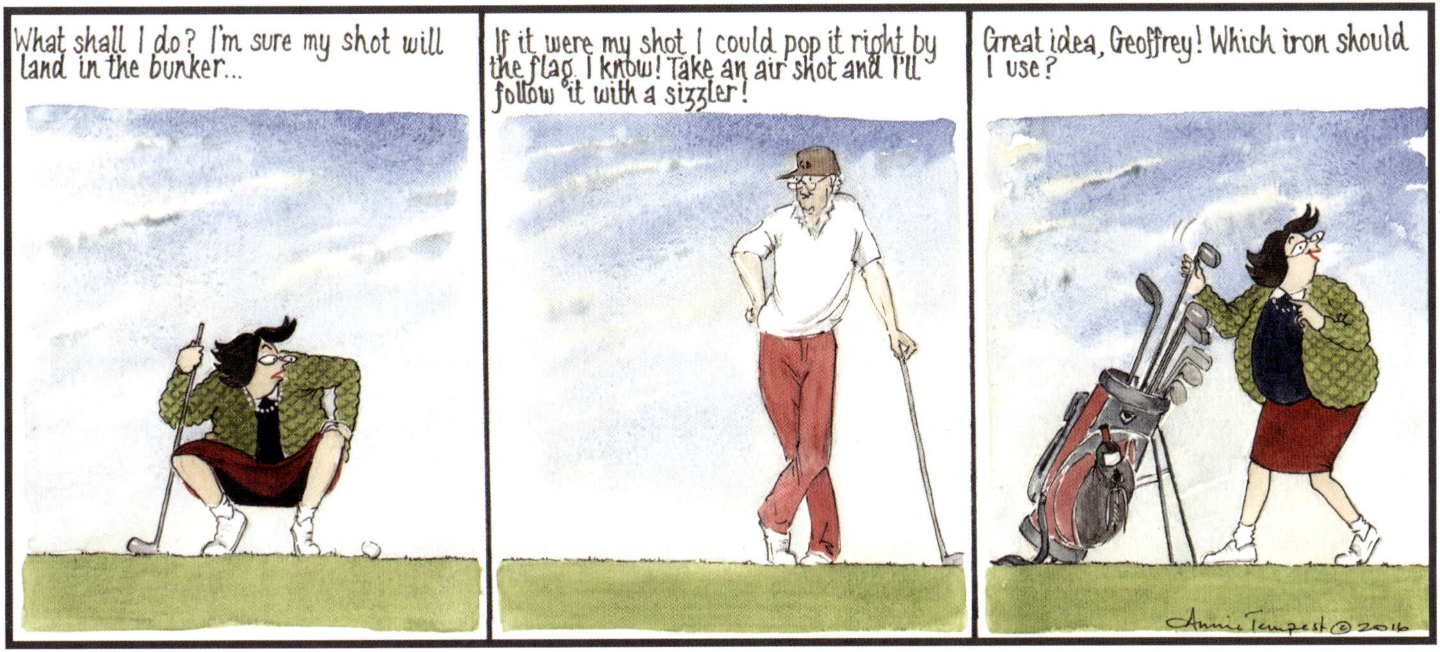
What shall I do? I'm sure my shot will land in the bunker...
If it were my shot I could pop it right by the flag. I know! Take an air shot and I'll follow it with a sizzler!
Great idea, Geoffrey! Which iron should I use?
Annie Tempest © 2016

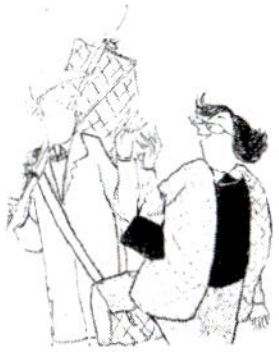

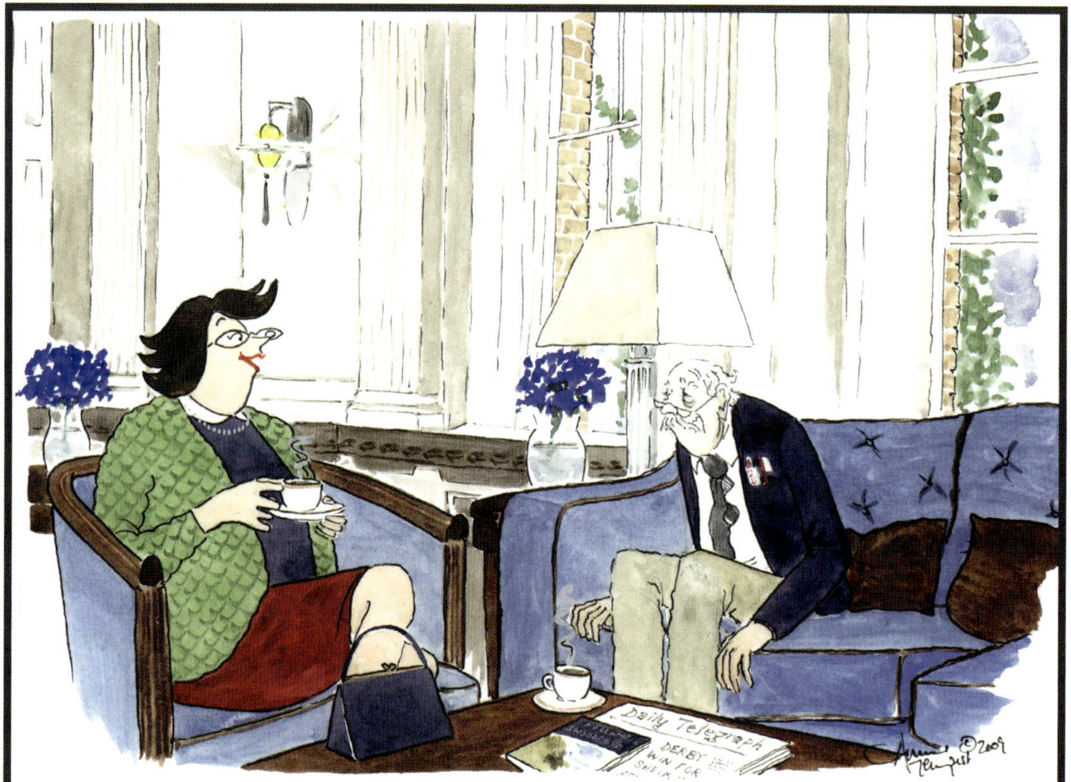
Daily Telegraph
DERBY
WIN FOR

"I take it you enjoyed the Golf Dinner last night, dear..."

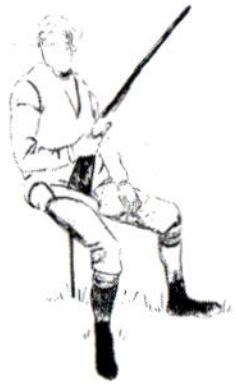

ANNIE TEMPEST © 2002

"I do think the Tissington-Tatlers overdo it a little..."

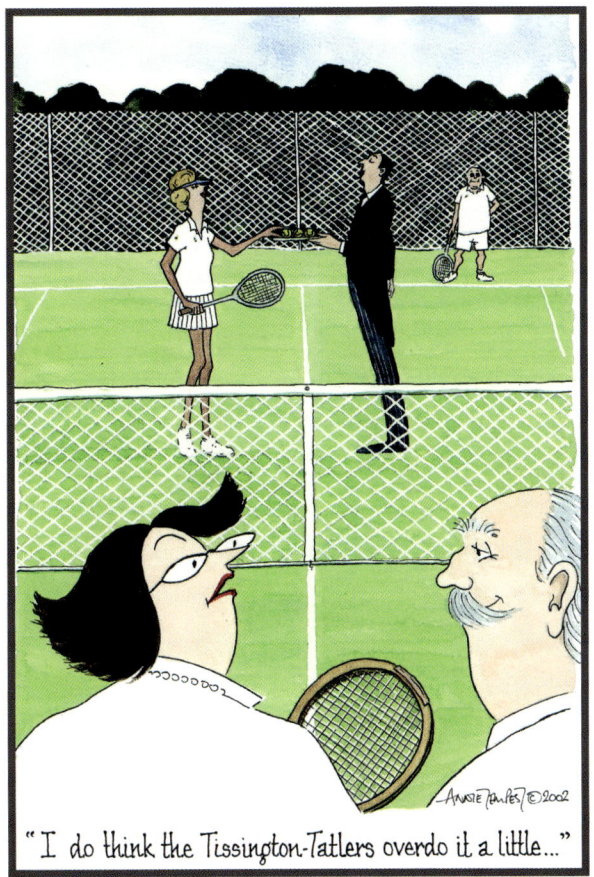

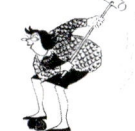

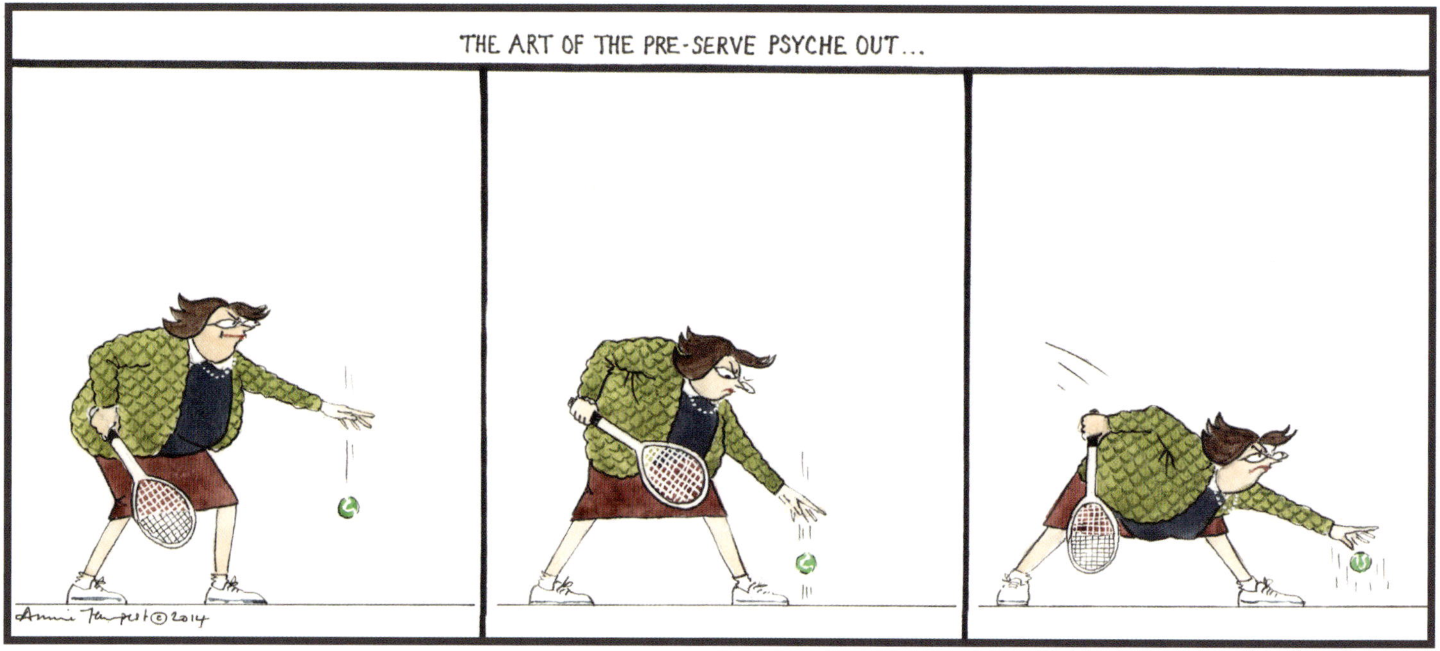
THE ART OF THE PRE-SERVE PSYCHE OUT...

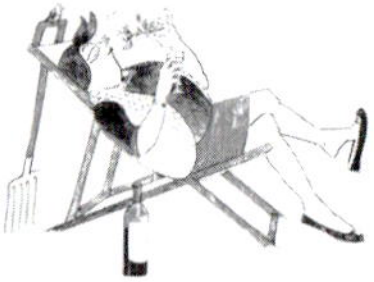

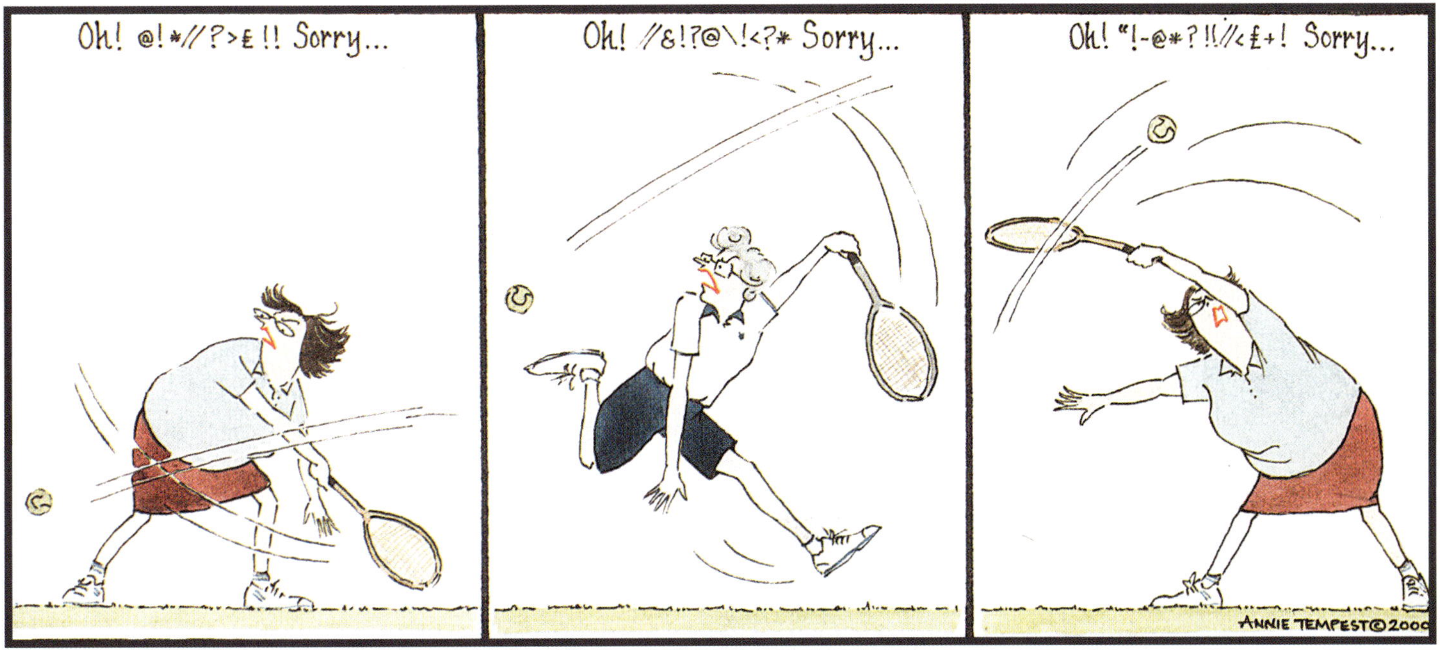
Oh! @!*//?>£!! Sorry...
Oh! //&!?@\!<?* Sorry...
Oh! "!-@*?!!//<£+! Sorry...
ANNIE TEMPEST©2000

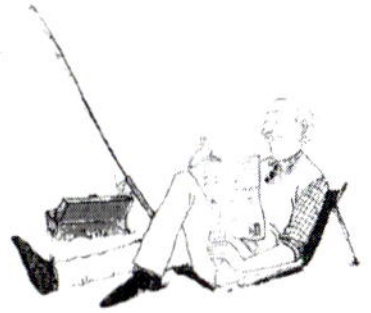

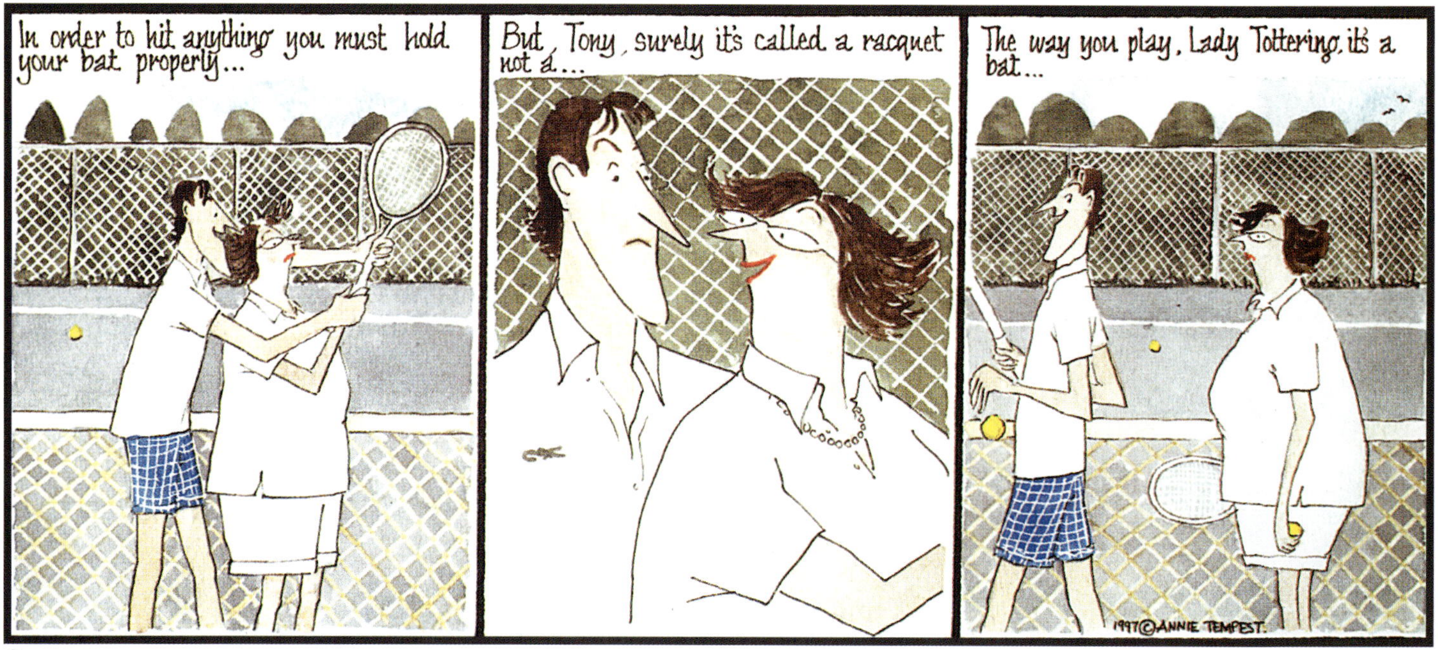
In order to hit anything you must hold your bat properly...
But, Tony, surely it's called a racquet not a...
The way you play, Lady Tottering, it's a bat...
1997 © ANNIE TEMPEST.

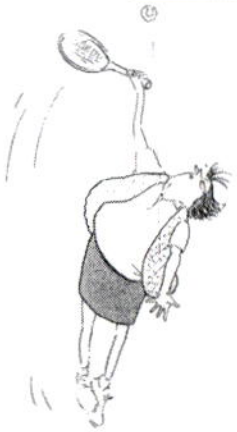

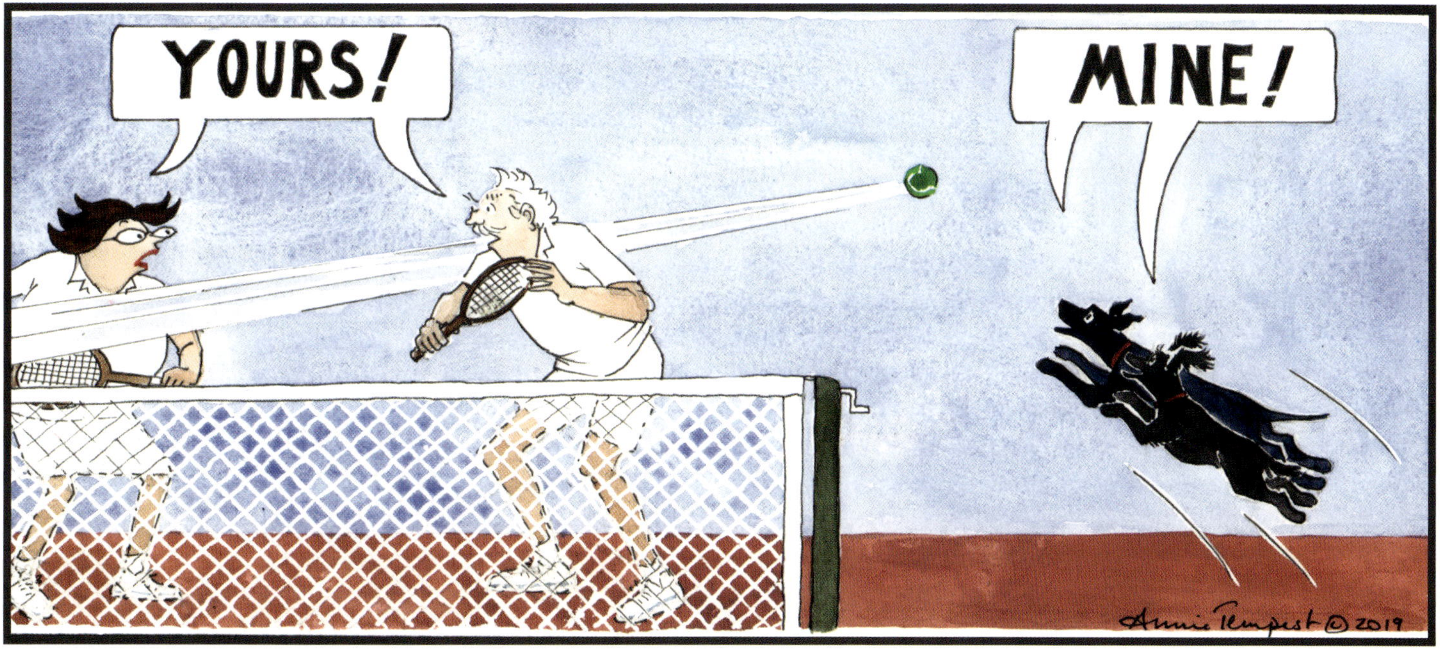
YOURS!
MINE!
Annie Tempest © 2019

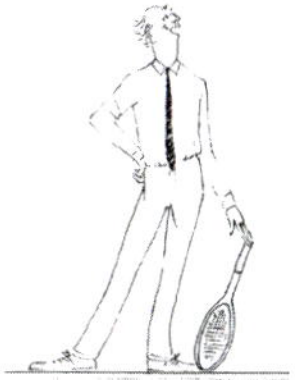

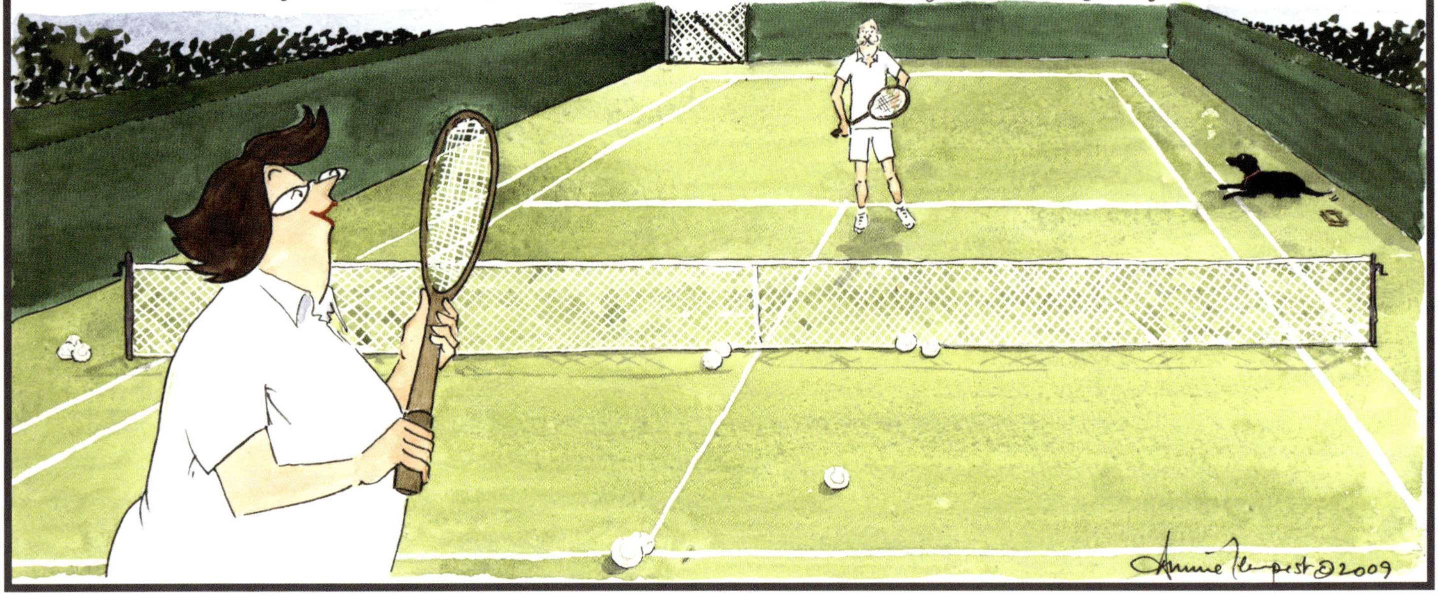
Annie Tempest ©2009

I did warn you that I was a bit of a Cinderella on the tennis court - odds are against me ever getting to the ball...

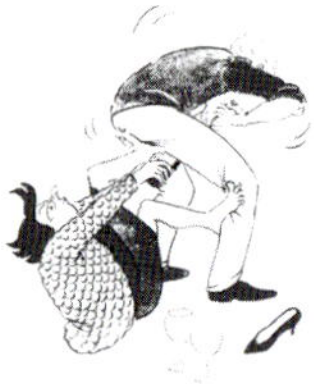

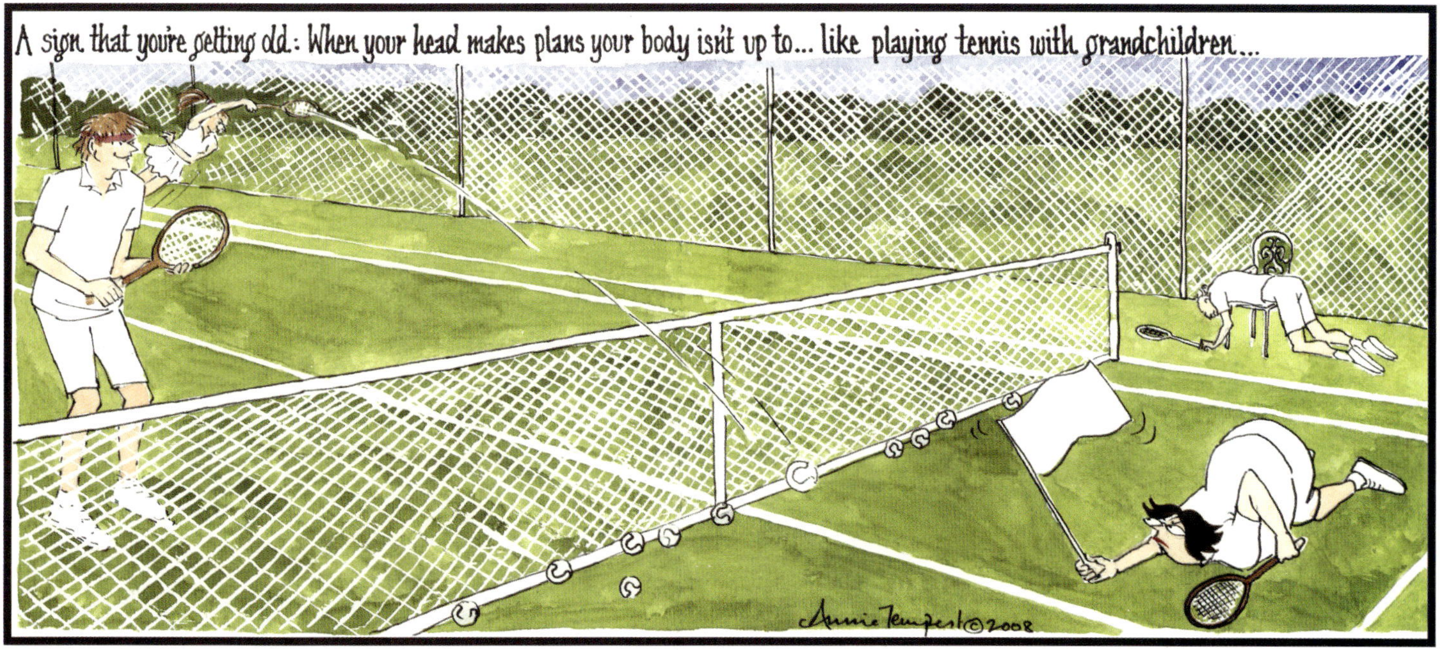
A sign that you're getting old: When your head makes plans your body isn't up to... like playing tennis with grandchildren...
Annie Tempest © 2008

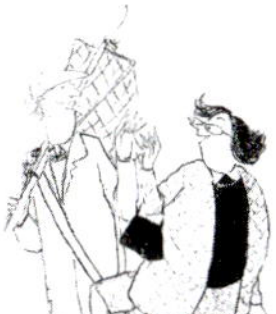

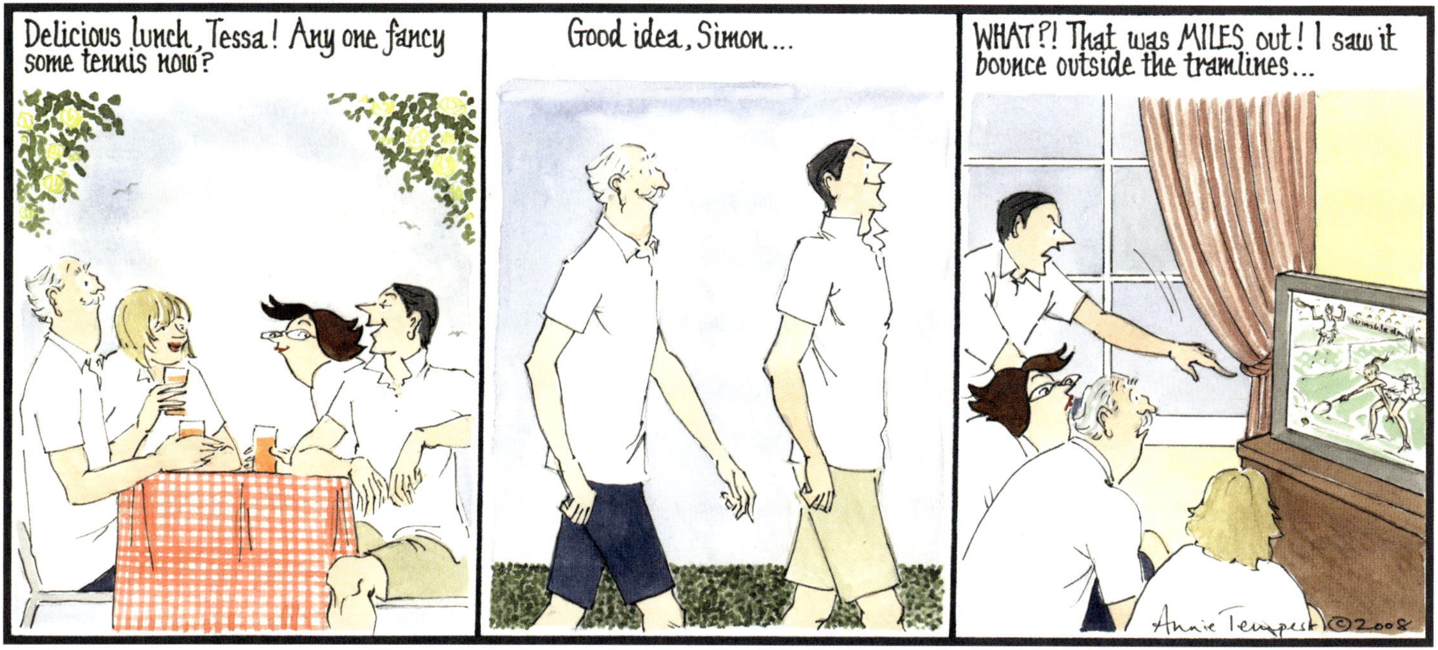
Delicious lunch, Tessa! Any one fancy some tennis now?
Good idea, Simon...
WHAT?! That was MILES out! I saw it bounce outside the tramlines...
Annie Tempest ©2008

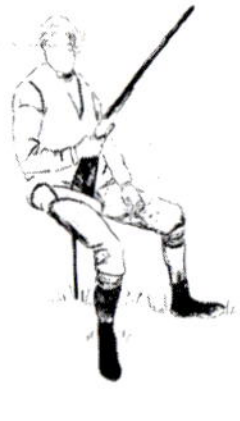

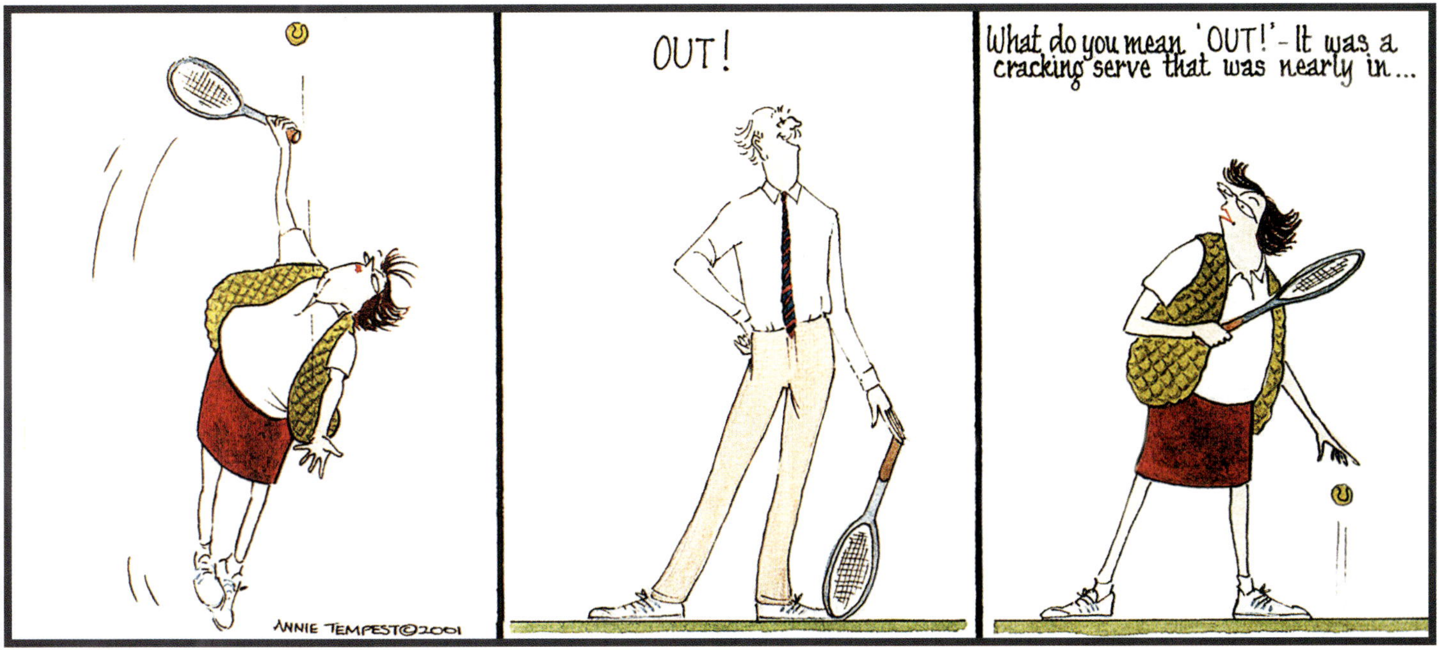
OUT!
What do you mean 'OUT!' - It was a cracking serve that was nearly in...
ANNIE TEMPEST©2001

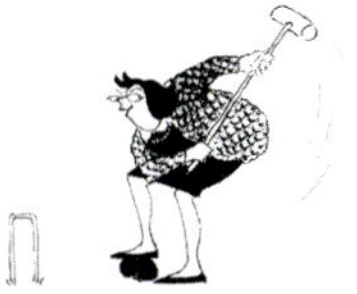

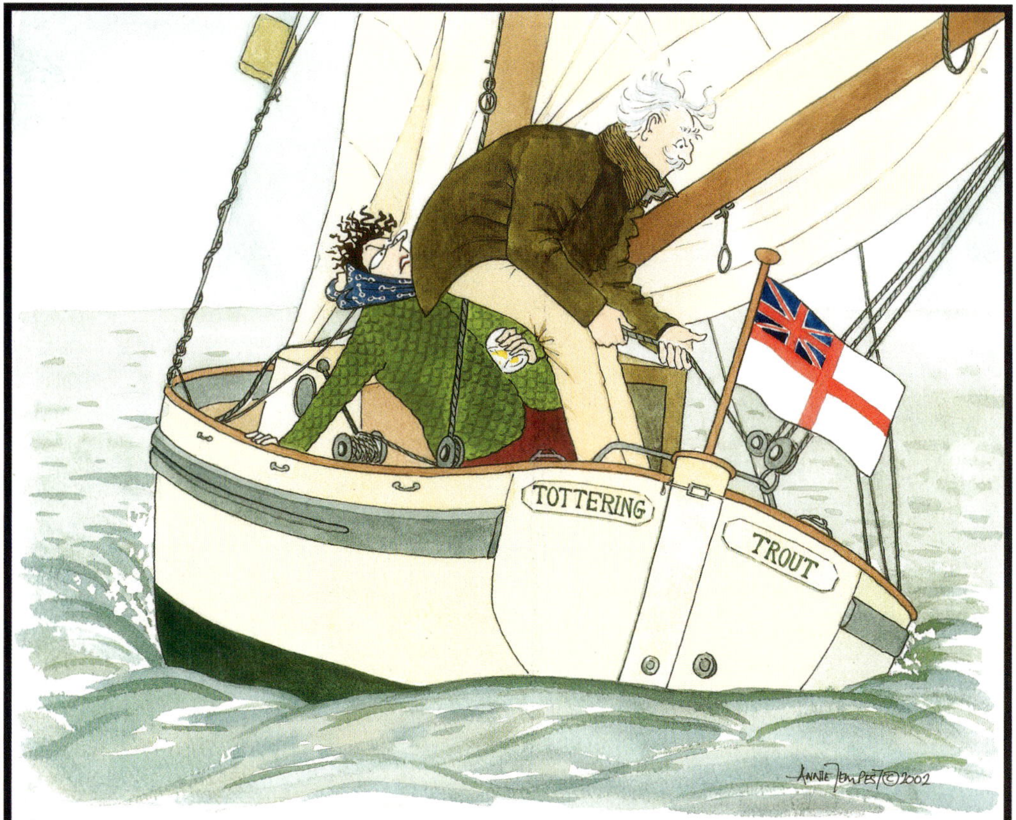
TOTTERING
TROUT
ANNIE TEMPEST © 2002

"What do you mean 'get a grip'? Your bum's in my face, you've spilt my gin and my hair's gone frizzy..."

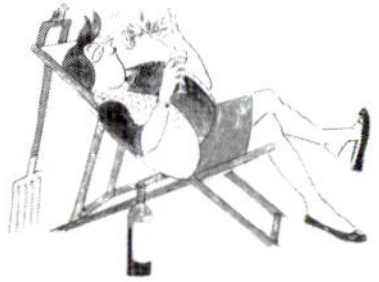

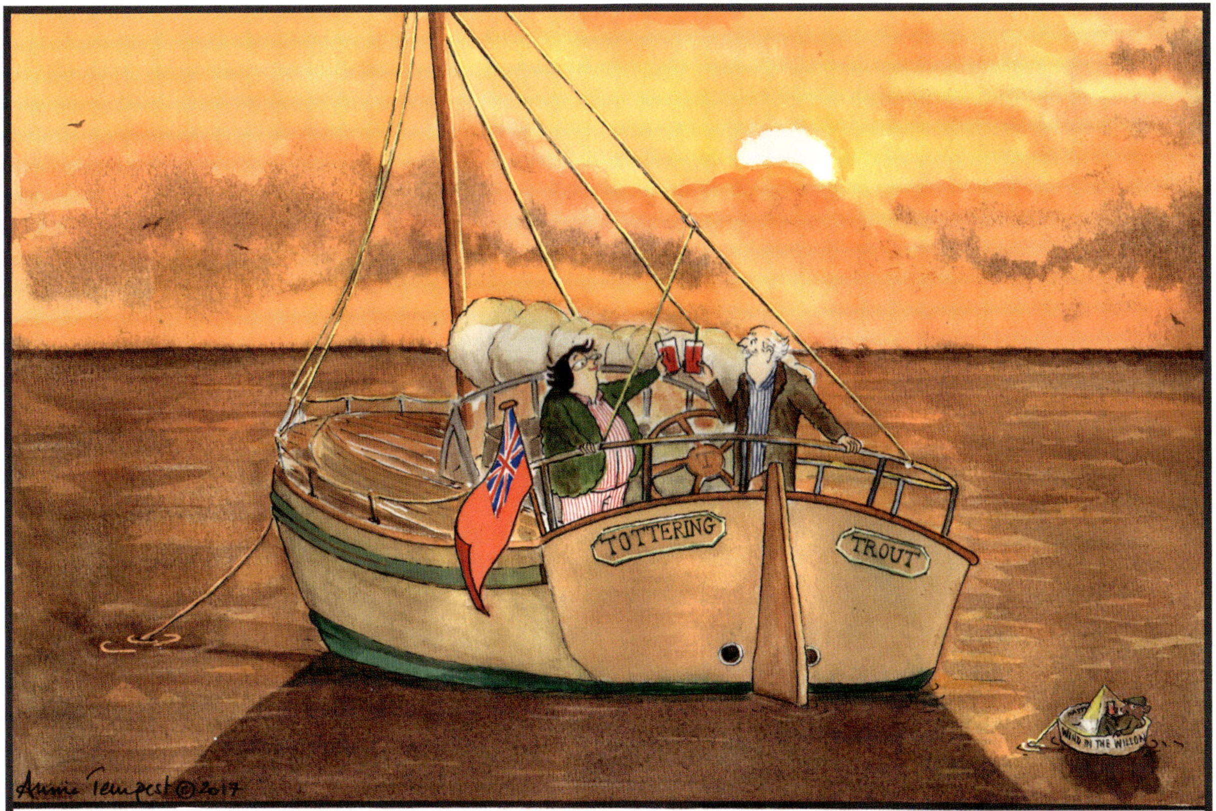
TOTTERING
TROUT
Annie Tempest © 2017

" A 'Morner' is a 'Nooner', only sooner... "

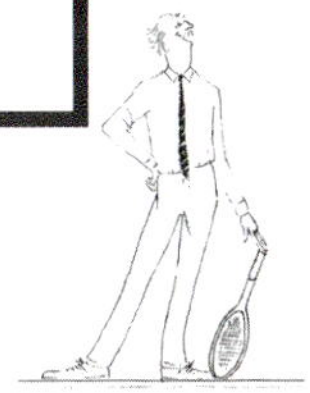

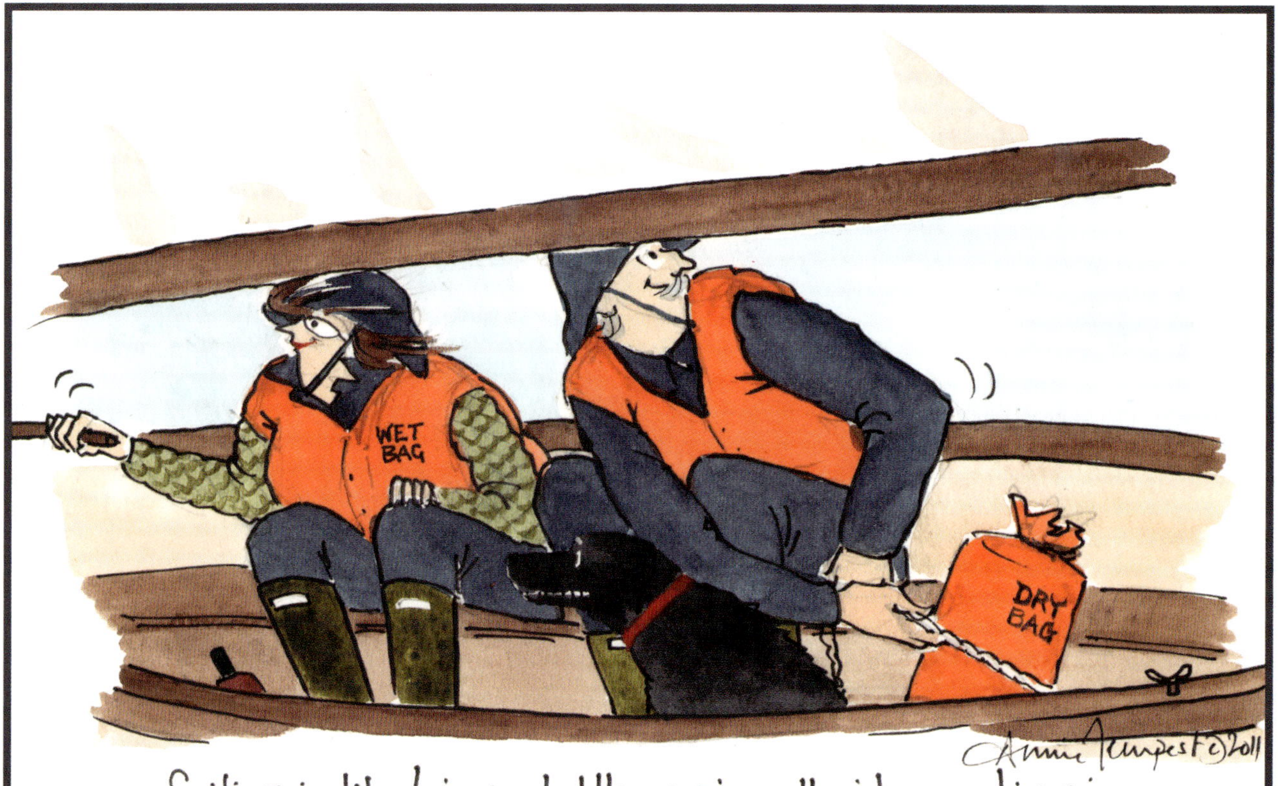
WET BAG
DRY BAG

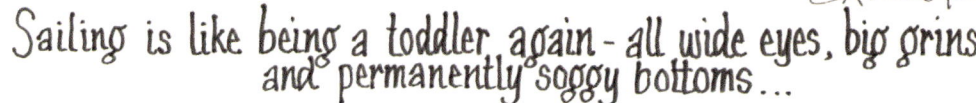

Sailing is like being a toddler again - all wide eyes, big grins and permanently soggy bottoms...

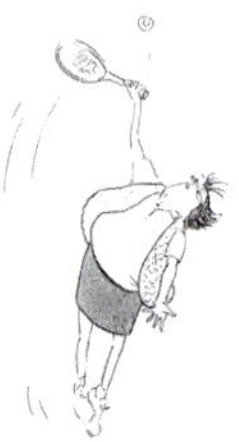

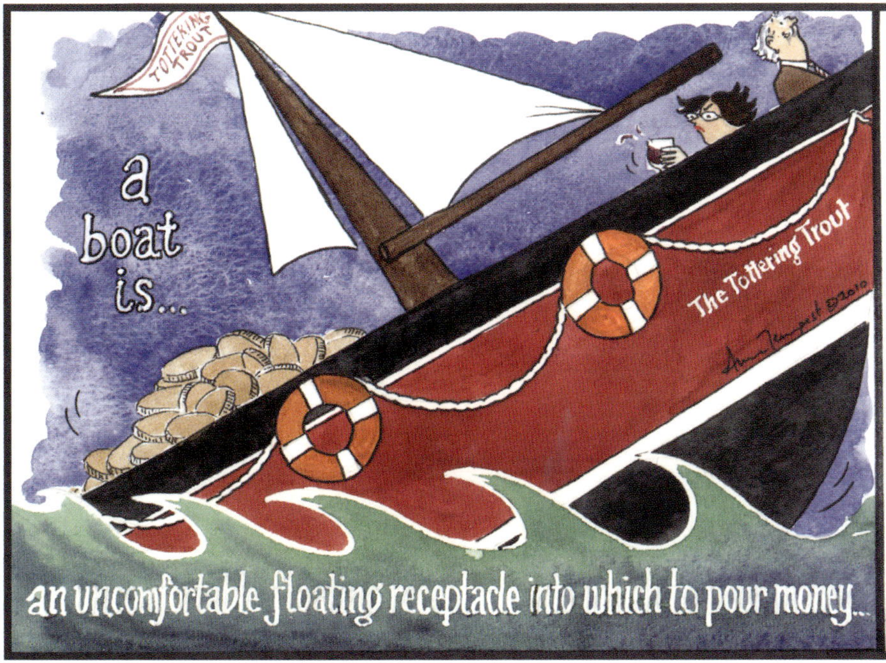
TOTTERING TROUT
a boat is...
The Tottering Trout
©2010
an uncomfortable floating receptacle into which to pour money...

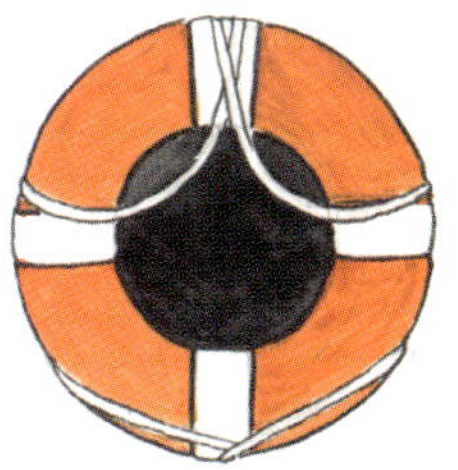

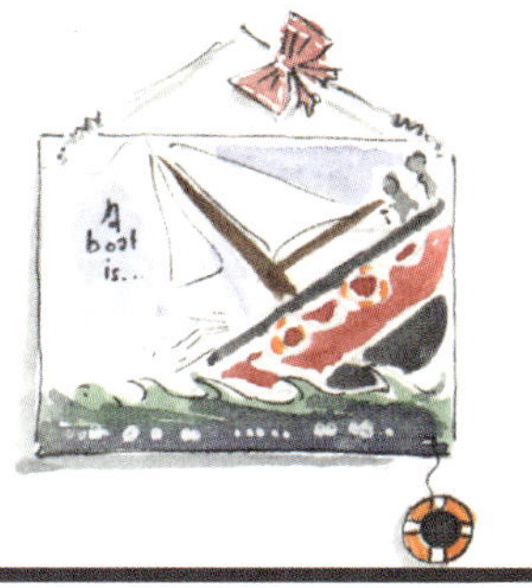
A boat is...

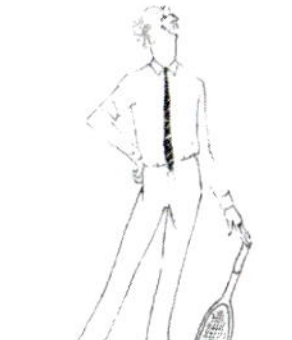

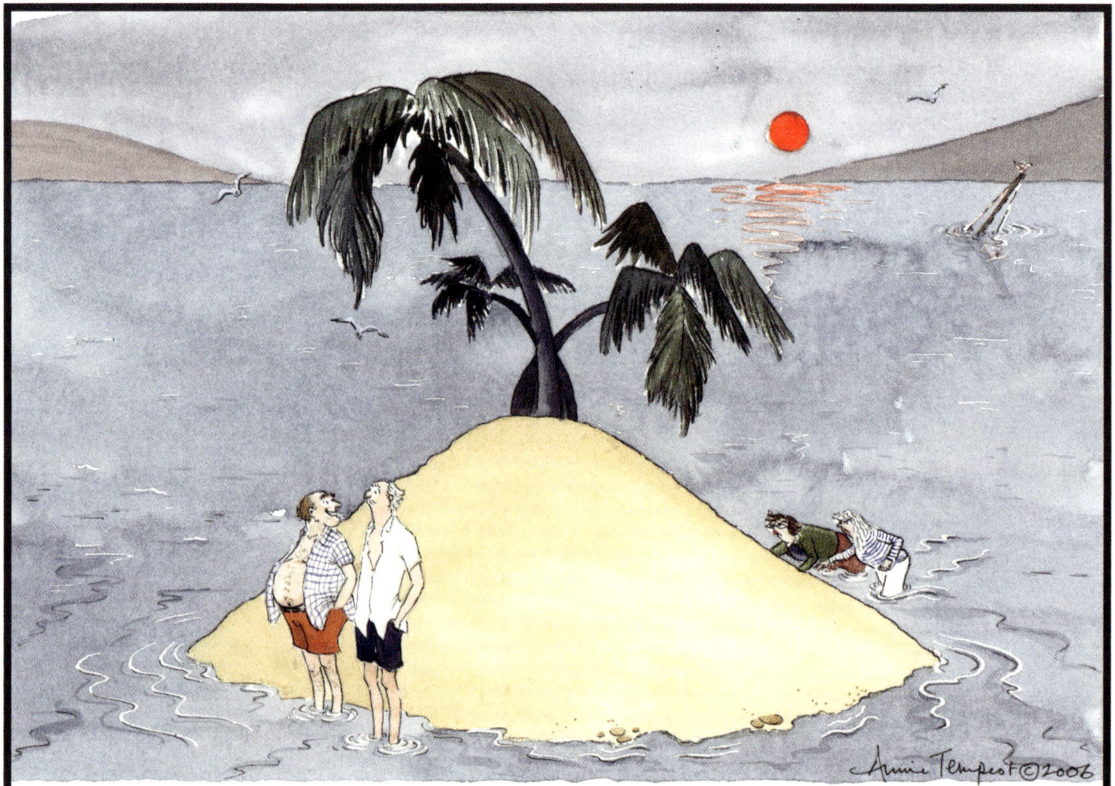
Annie Tempest ©2006

'Let's look on the bright side - at least we'll never have to hear "I told you so..." '

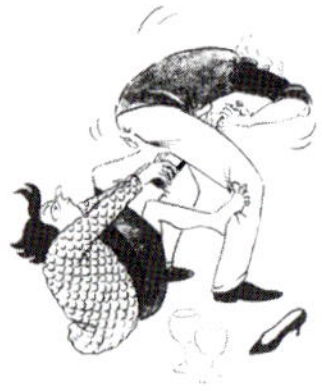

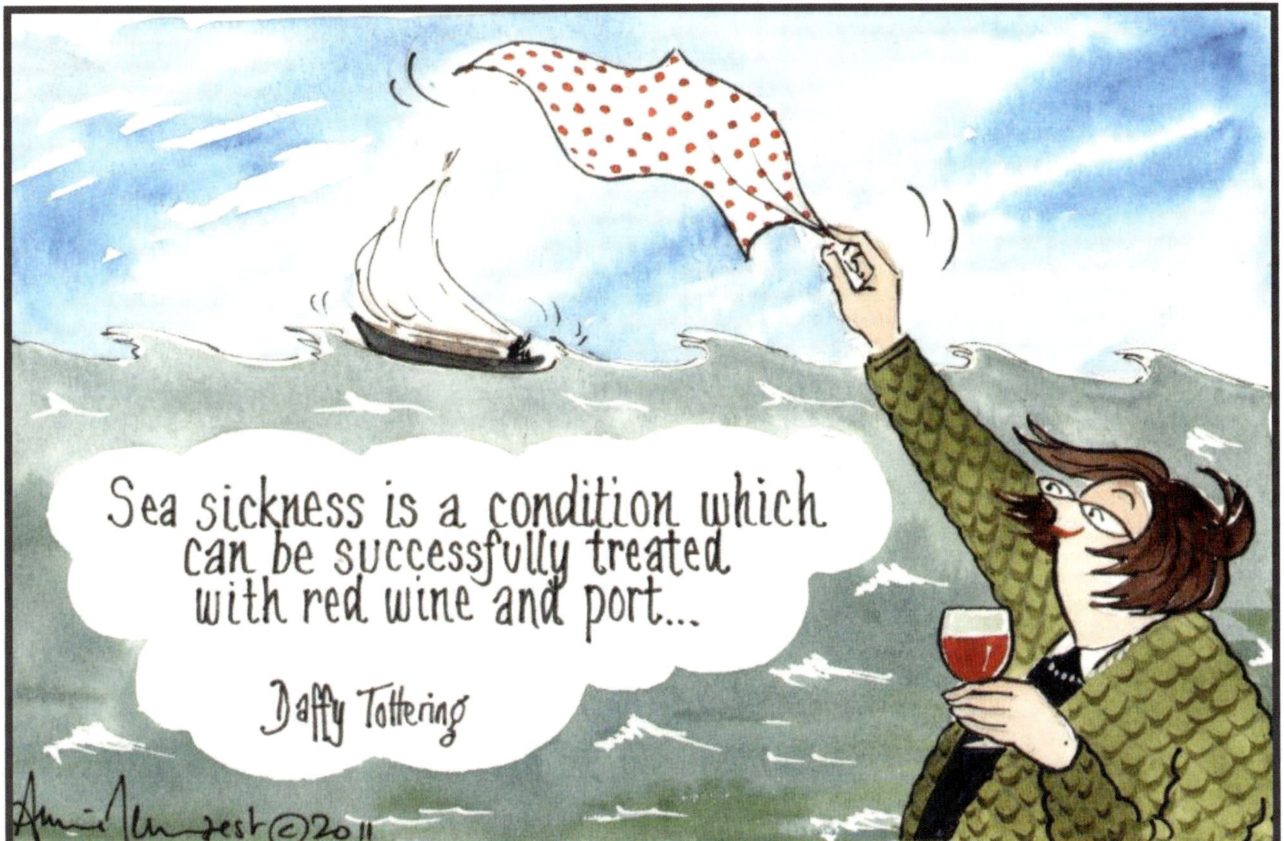
Sea sickness is a condition which
can be successfully treated
with red wine and port...
Daffy Tottering
©2011

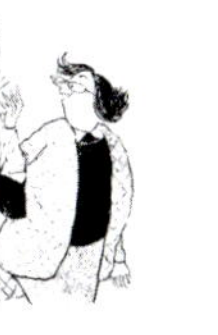

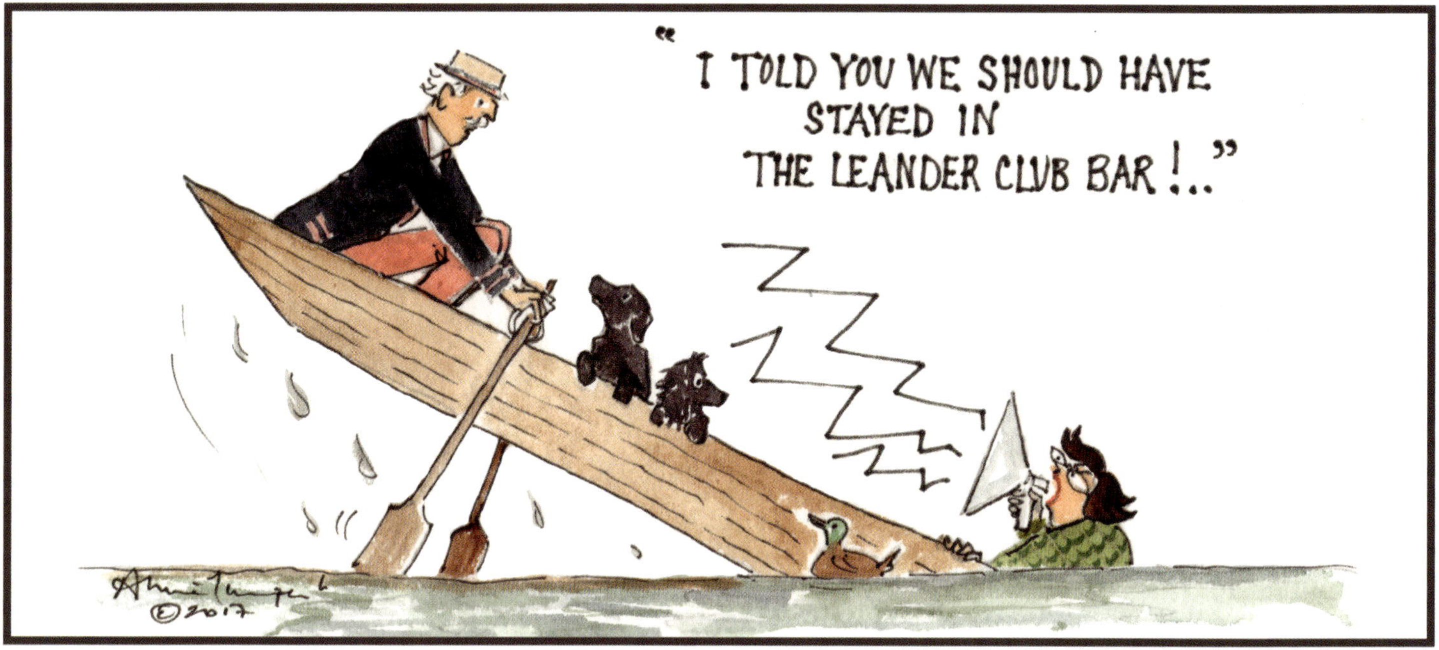
"I TOLD YOU WE SHOULD HAVE STAYED IN THE LEANDER CLUB BAR!.."
©2017

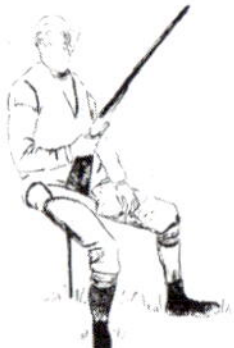

Nautical Daffynitions...

Annie Tempest ©2003

Bow thruster...
Taking a reef...
Dead reckoning...
A grab-bag...

A gybe...

A running fix...
Heaving to...
Tacking...
Casting off...

Splicing the mainbrace...

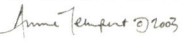

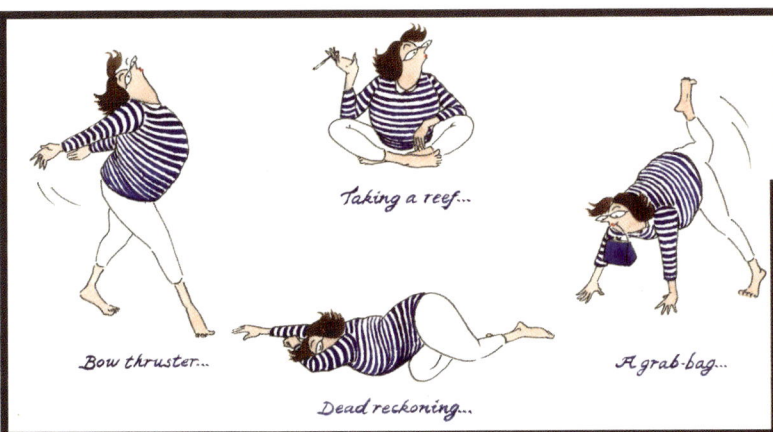

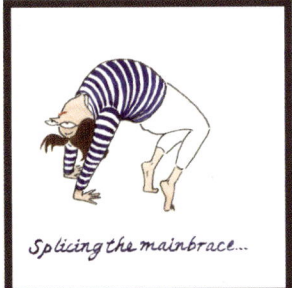

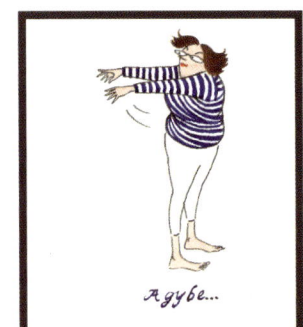

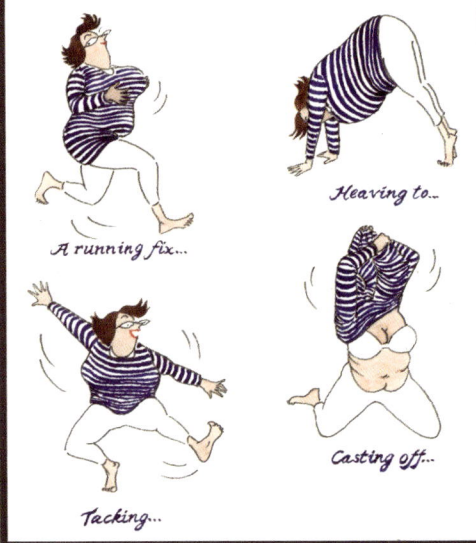

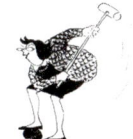

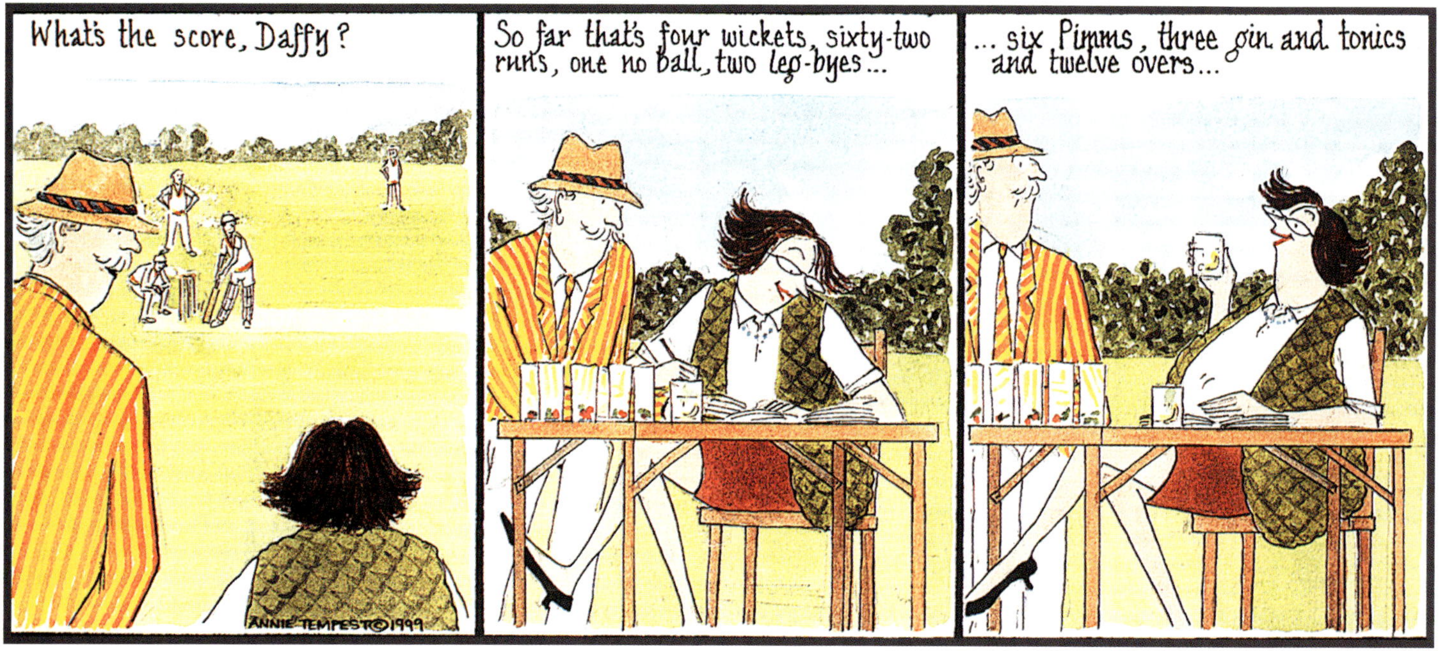
What's the score, Daffy?
So far that's four wickets, sixty-two runs, one no ball, two leg-byes...
... six Pimms, three gin and tonics and twelve overs...
ANNIE TEMPEST © 1999

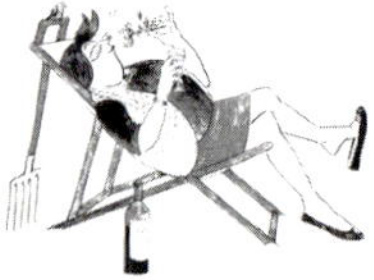

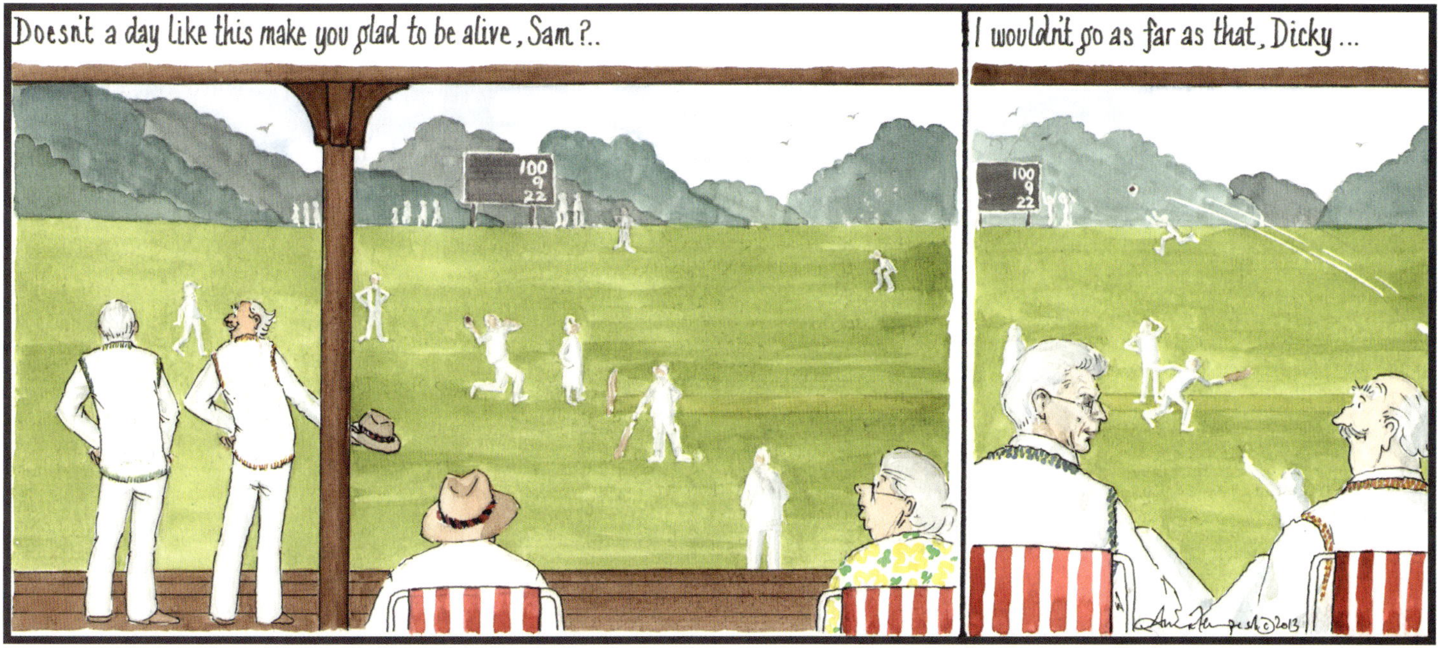
Doesn't a day like this make you glad to be alive, Sam?..
100
9
22
I wouldn't go as far as that, Dicky...
100
9
22

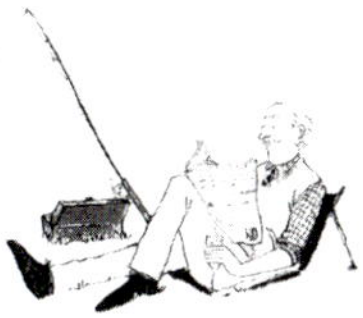

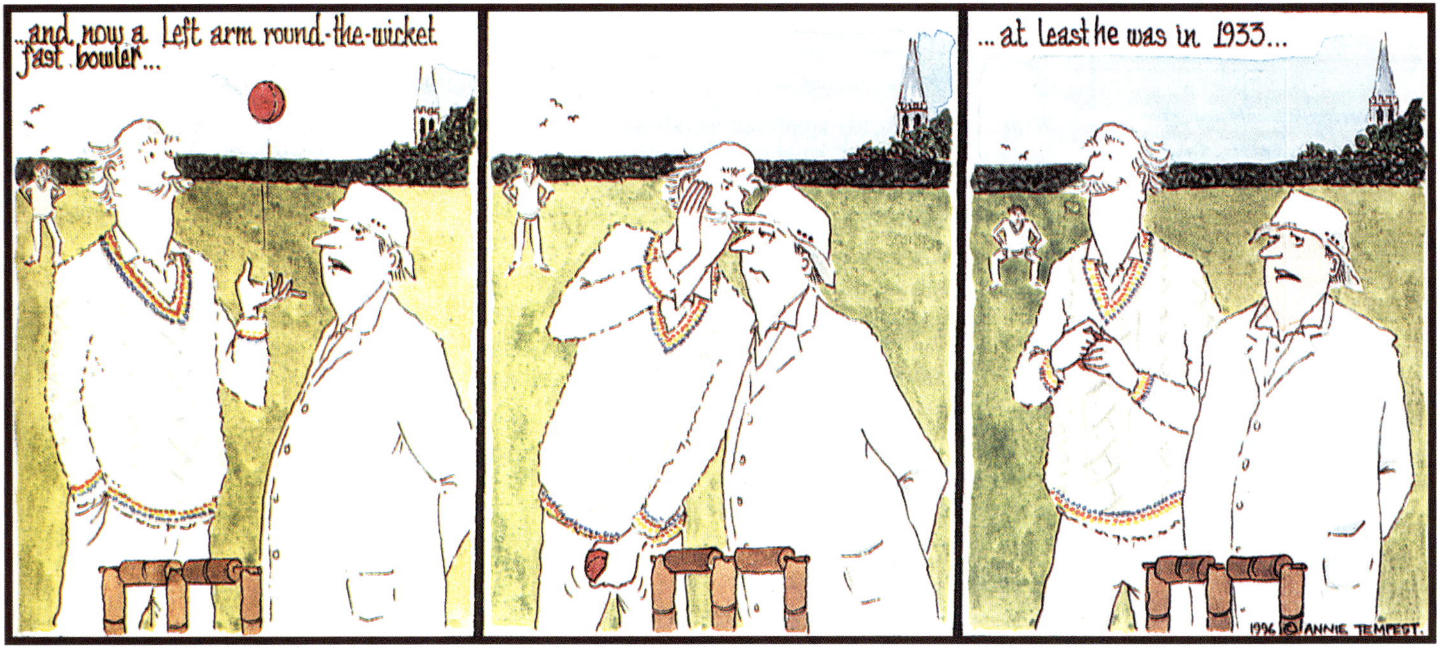
...and now a Left arm round-the-wicket fast bowler...
... at least he was in 1933...
1996 © ANNIE TEMPEST.

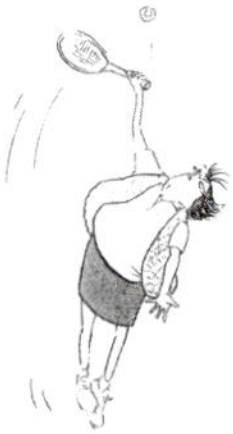

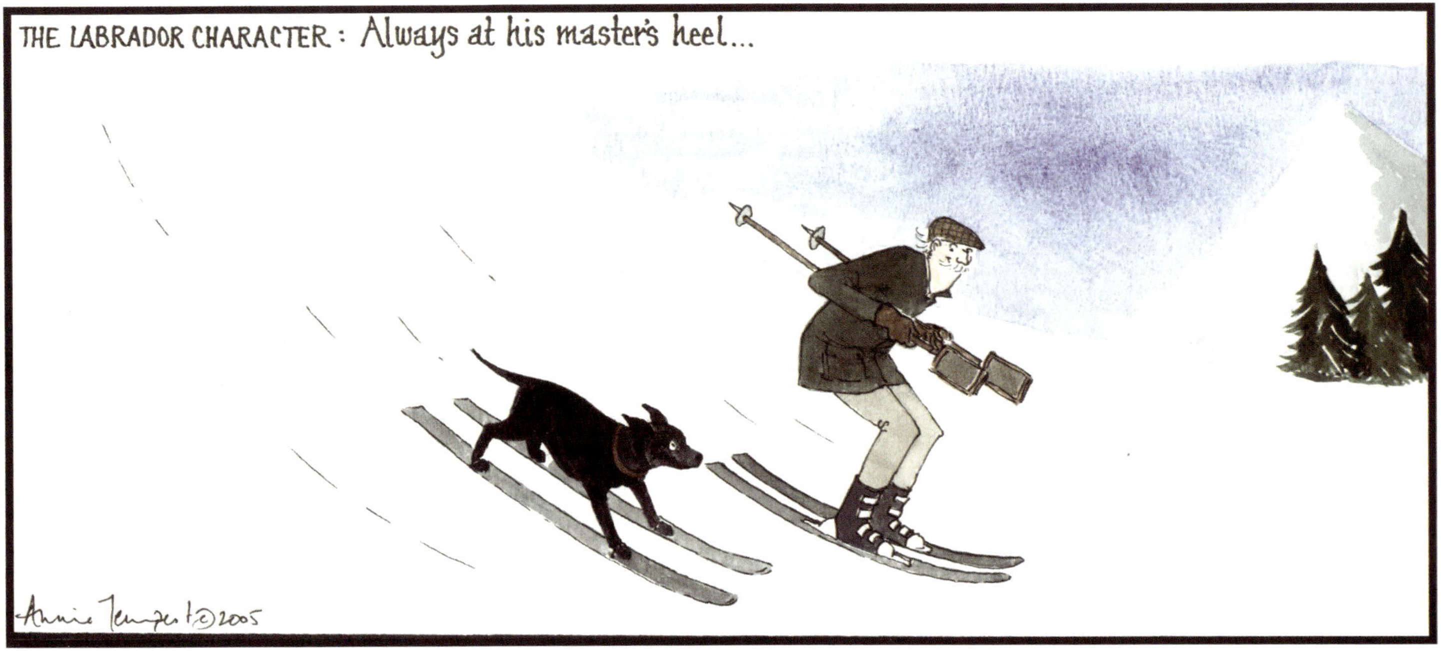
THE LABRADOR CHARACTER : Always at his master's heel...
Annie Tempest ©2005

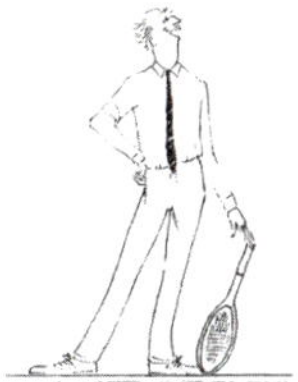

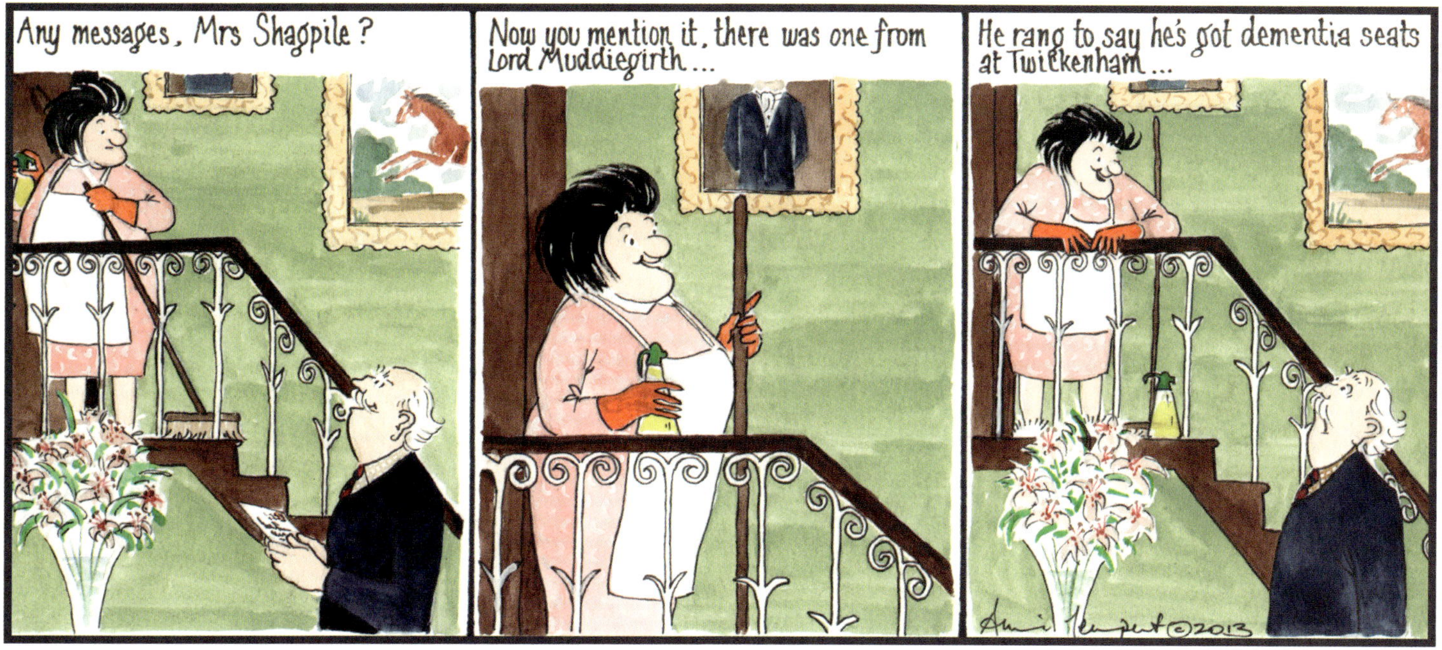
Any messages, Mrs Shagpile?
Now you mention it, there was one from Lord Muddiegirth...
He rang to say he's got dementia seats at Twickenham...

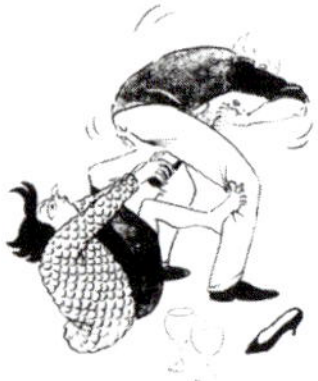

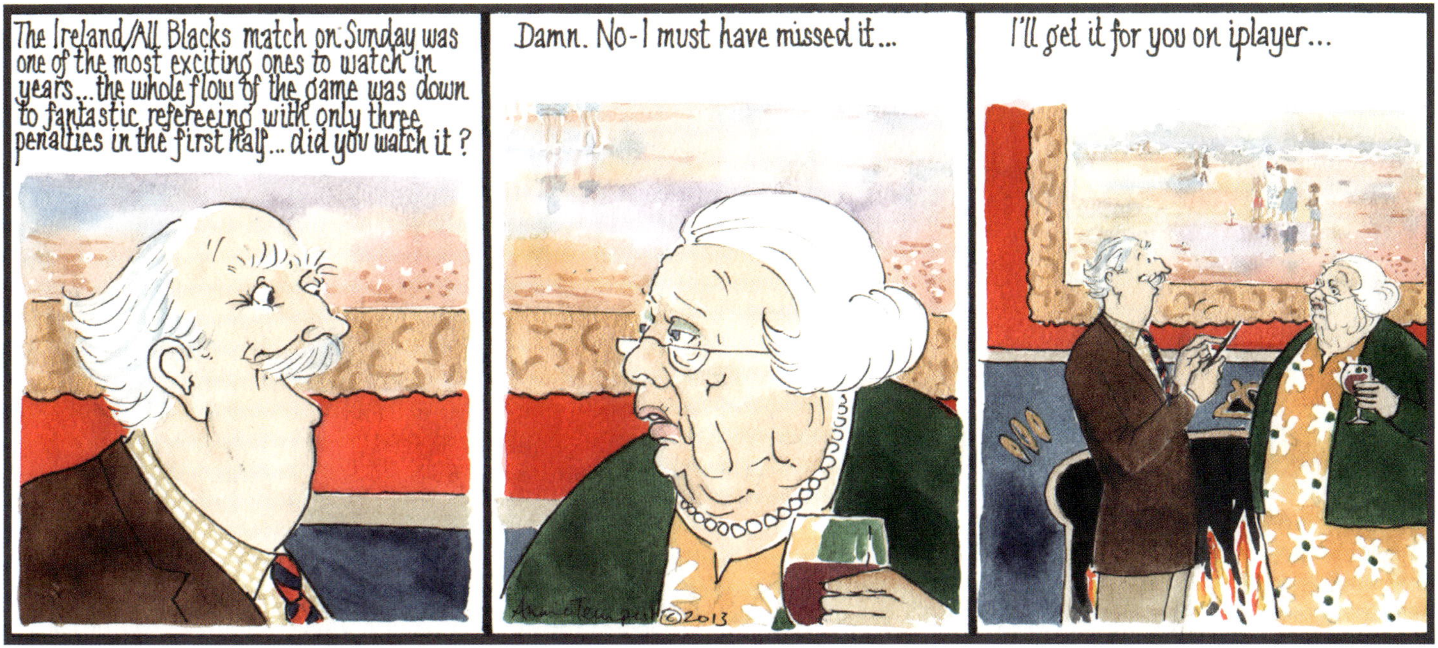
The Ireland/All Blacks match on Sunday was one of the most exciting ones to watch in years... the whole flow of the game was down to fantastic refereeing with only three penalties in the first half... did you watch it ?
Damn. No-I must have missed it...
I'll get it for you on iplayer...

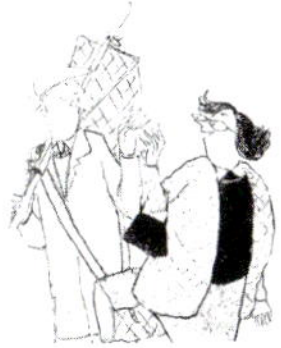

June

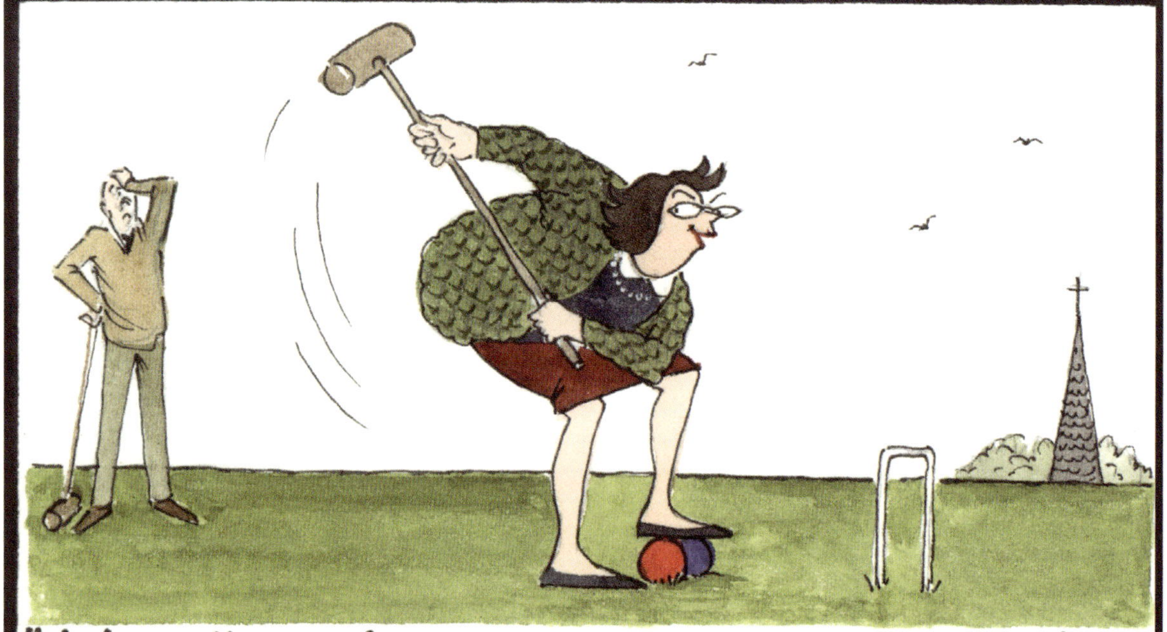

" I hope the windows are insured on your village church..."

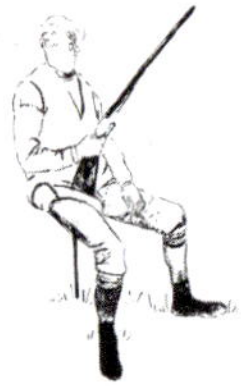

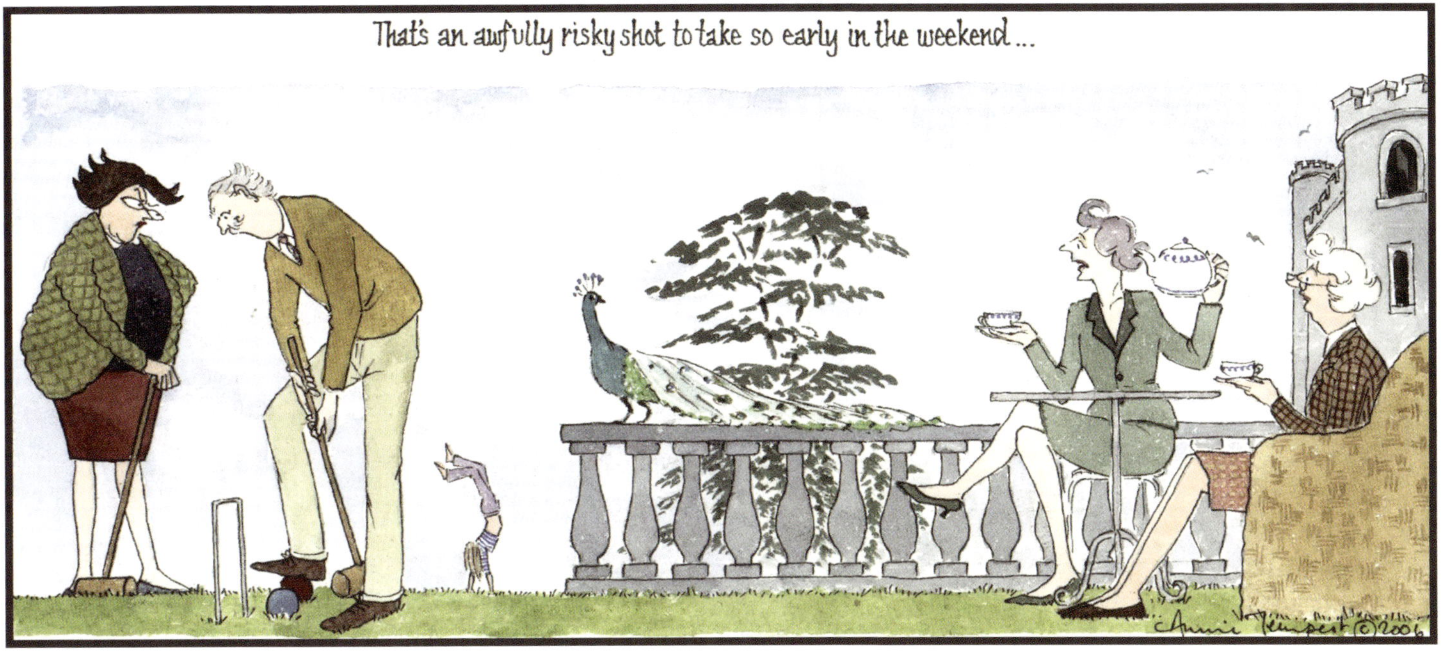

That's an awfully risky shot to take so early in the weekend ...

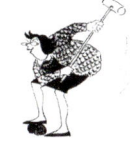

'Silence at all times' is proving a little taxing for some of our senior members...

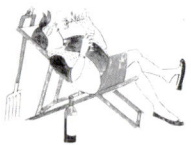

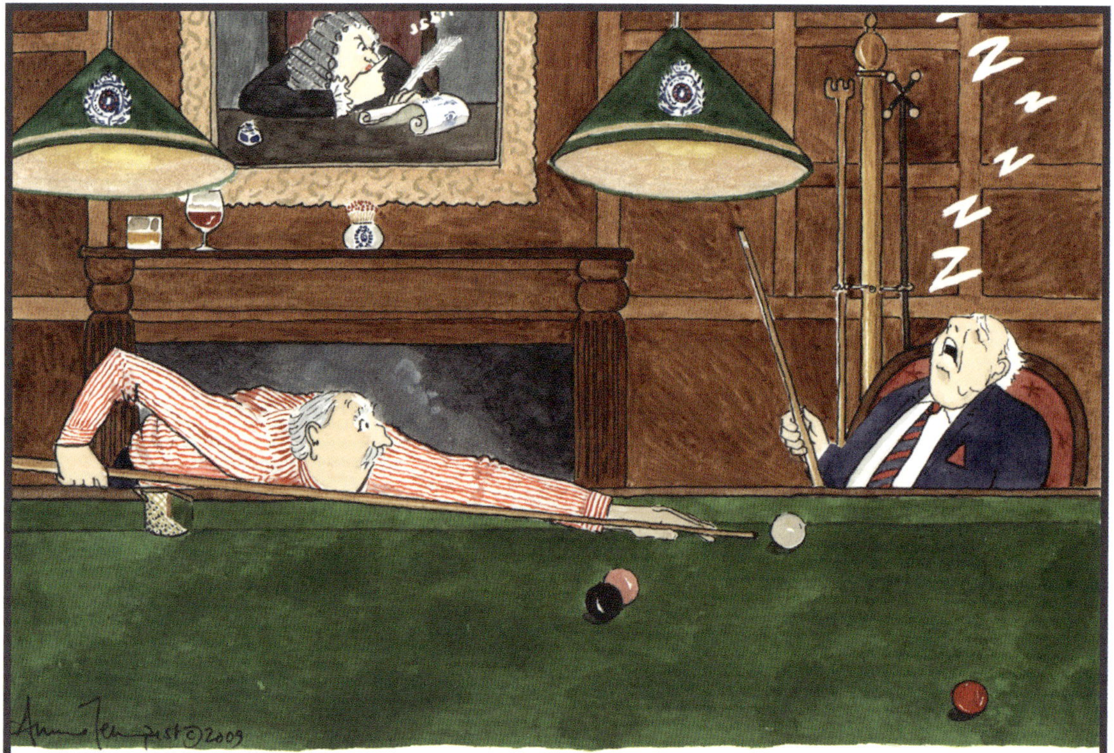

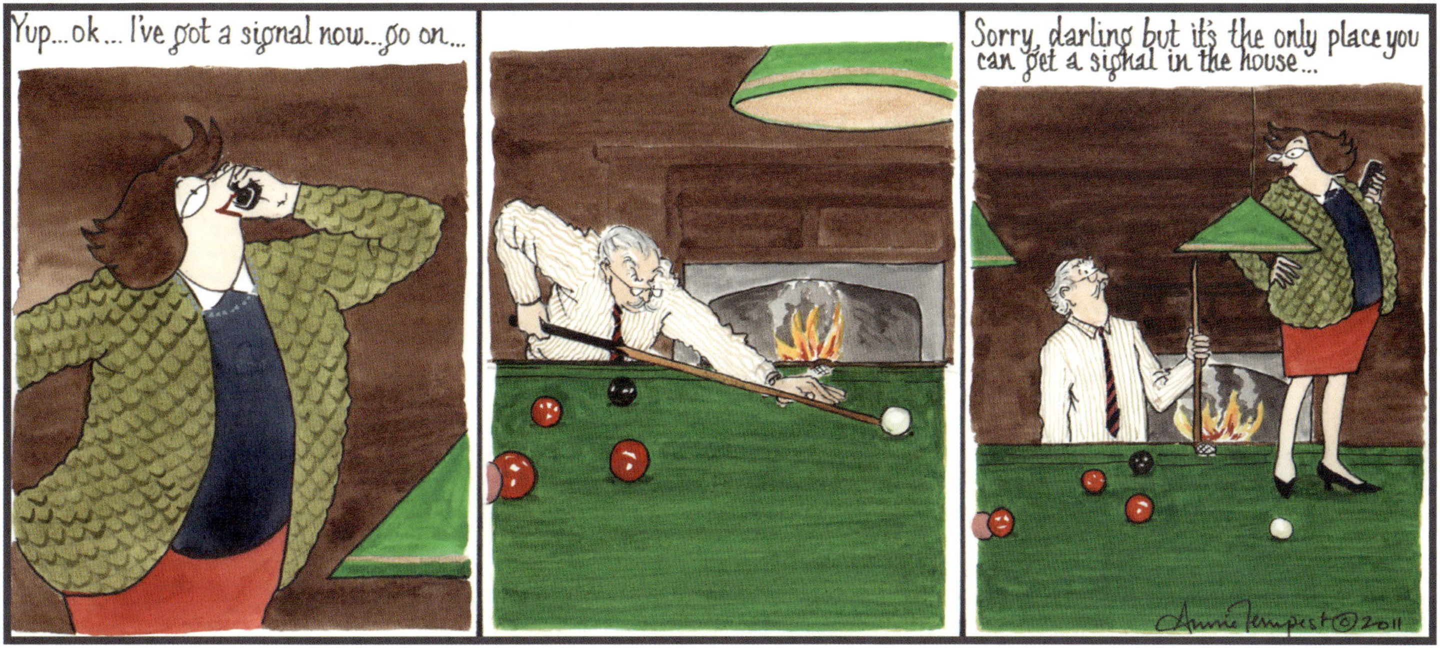
Yup... ok... I've got a signal now... go on...
Sorry, darling but it's the only place you can get a signal in the house...
Annie Tempest © 2011

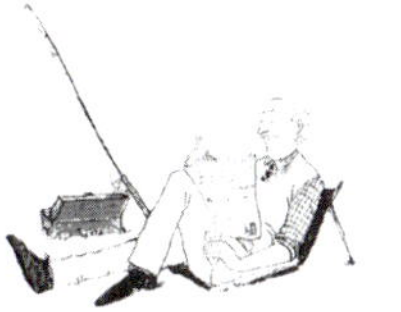

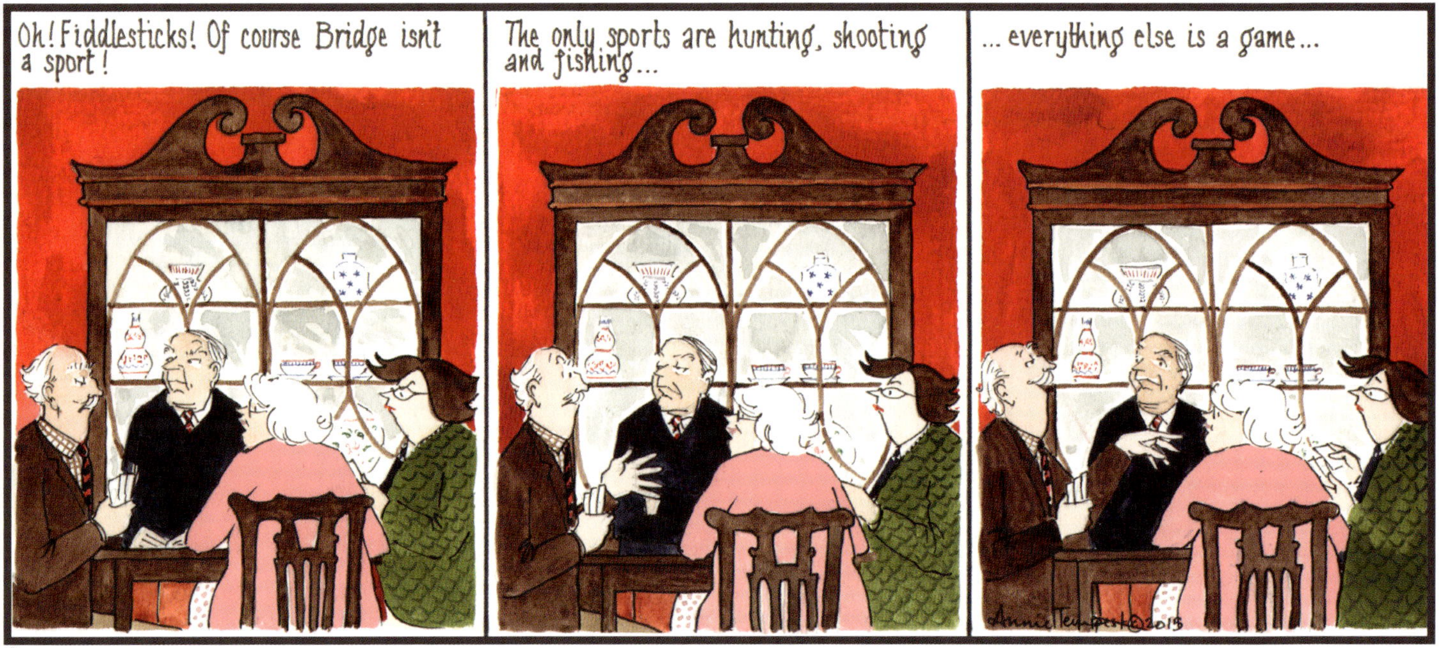
Oh! Fiddlesticks! Of course Bridge isn't a sport!
The only sports are hunting, shooting and fishing...
... everything else is a game...
Annie Tempest © 2013

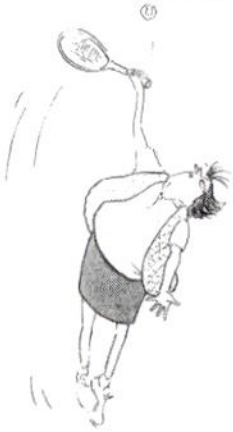

Jane and I thought it would be rather fun to play girls against boys for a change...

Anne Tempest ©2006

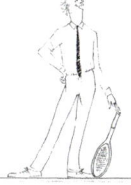

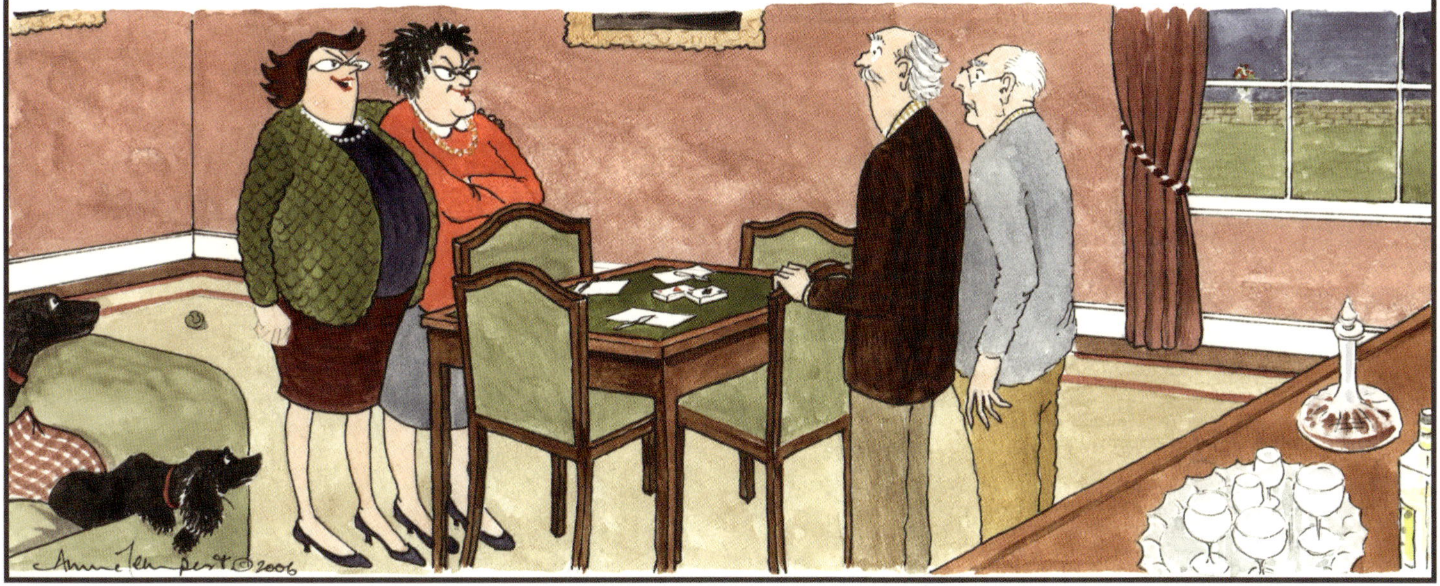

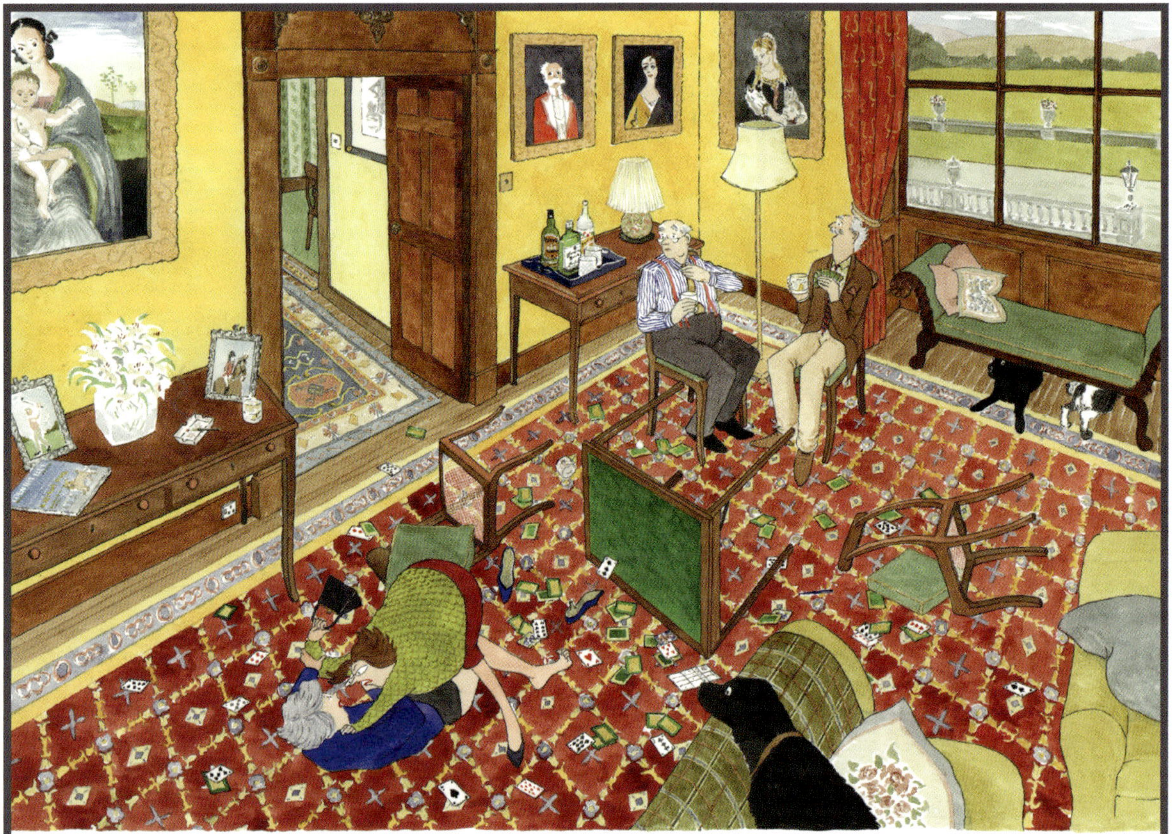

"I did warn you that my wife was rather a competitive Bridge player and, after all, Caroline did revoke..."

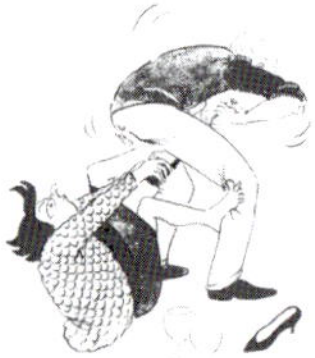

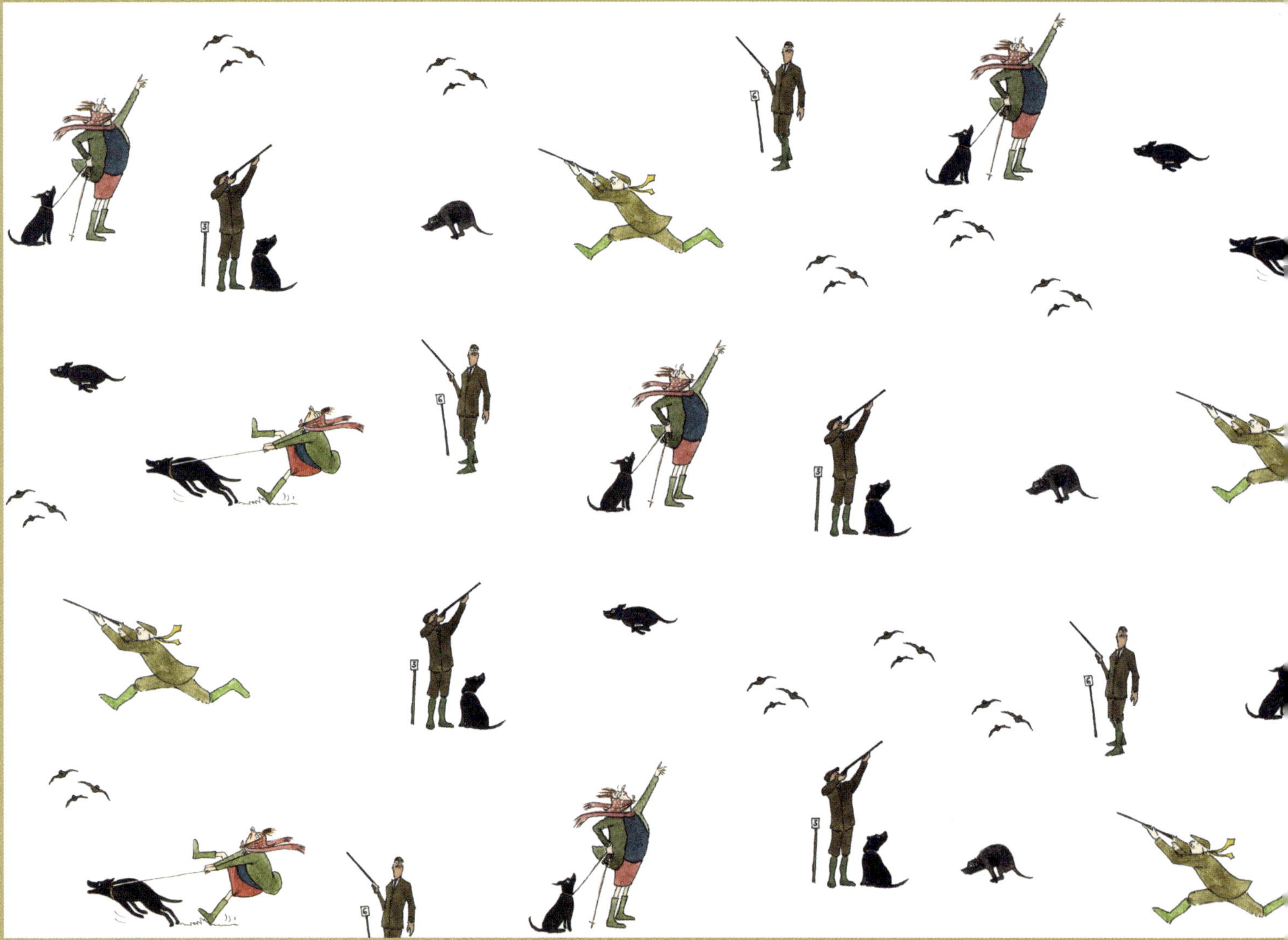